ANGELS: BEINGS OF LIGHT
The Wisdom and Teachings of
God's Messengers on Earth

Blessings,
Linda Porter

ANGELS: BEINGS OF LIGHT
The Wisdom and Teachings of
God's Messengers on Earth

Linda Porter
And
Us

Ascential Publishing Inc.
South Bend, Indiana

Ascential Publishing Inc.
P.O. Box 4132
South Bend, IN 46634
E-mail: ascentialbooks@aol.com
web: www.ascentialpublishing.com

Cover and artistic design by Matt Porter
Stellar Creative • www.stellarcreative.com

Library of Congress Control Number: 2001117625

ISBN 0-9710616-0-2

Printed in the United States of America

First Edition

This book is dedicated to God, our Creator and Sustainer.

It is also dedicated in memory of and with love and honor to Kevin Zeiler, who touched many lives during his life, and will touch many more in death.
Thank you.

WORDS OF THANKS

There are so many people to thank for their contributions during the unfolding of this book.

First, I wish to thank God for the Divine Love and abundant blessings I have been given.

I wish to thank my angels and guides for their love, encouragement, and patience, without which there would be no book. I am honored by their trust in me and can only pray that I have presented their words and teachings as accurately as possible. They have blessed my life inordinately, and I am eternally grateful.

Much love and gratitude goes to my family:

—my sons and daughter-in-law—Alex Porter, Mathew Porter, and Colleen Riley. Along with such loving support, they have all participated in many tangible ways—book cover design, artistic design, publishing name, web site design, proof-reading, business advice, and a willing ear, to name just a few. They are such incredible blessings in my life.

—my mother and stepfather—Alice and Don Baker, who believed in me from the outset and continued their belief as things got progressively "stranger." Their steadfastness is more appreciated than they'll ever know.

—my father-in-law—Victor Porter for his belief and encouragement and my mother-in-law—Kristine Porter for her great command of the English language and the gift of her proof-reading.

—my brother-in-law—Charlie Brune and his sister Katie for their wonderful printing service. Charlie understood our vision and helped us attain it.

Special thanks goes to my dearest friend, Vicky Stickley-Freeman, who no matter what I told her or asked her, went with it, and encouraged me to believe that with God anything is possible—anything! She's right. Many thanks.
Thanks also to her husband, Jon, for his willingness to listen and the encouragement he provided.

There are numerous women in my life who deserve special thanks. They come in all ages and have given me such tremendous support during this endeavor. They are probably not aware of how much they have done for me, but I know. Here they are: Cindy Adamsson, Kerri Atkinson, Rylin and Tamara Bagarus, Doris Brown, Diana Green, Sue Jebelian, Genelle King, Sandy Kronewitter, Amelia McCready, Patti McCready, Ruth Lash, Lyn Mischel, Pat Mitchell, Virginia O'Hair, Cindy Pavel, Bonnie Riley, Dr. Marie Udulutch, Mary Welsheimer, and Sara Wood.

I wish to thank my Sunday School class—the Koinonia Class. They sat patiently by as I explored concepts unfamiliar to them, such as reincarnation. I owe them much gratitude.
I also need to thank the congregation of First United

Methodist Church of South Bend. They have given me much love and support for many years. To our new minister, Rev. Daniel Berger, I am so grateful for the new life he is bringing to our church, and for the ideals of tolerance and acceptance that he espouses.

Ike Lash has to be singled out for his incredible support. He will never know the impact of his belief in me. I so treasure our friendship.

And now for my spiritual comrades—the group that spun out from Barnes and Noble Spirituality Readers—Joy Wilkinson, Eric Bond, and Paul Pasman. The times I spend with them are such growth experiences. They have all three touched my heart, my mind, and my soul. And Eric—has gone way beyond the call to duty. Words can not express the gratitude I feel for his support, his encouragement, and his willingness to process whatever I come to him with. He is wise far beyond his years. Bless him.

Many thanks to Shelia Shumate, the Angelic Light Worker from Sedona, Arizona. The guidance she has passed on to me has been so very important during this process. Plus she, herself, has been such an inspiration to me. From her, I have learned what an Angelic Light Worker should be. I thank her for the fine example. Many blessings on her.

I would be remiss without thanking the staff at Borders Café. They provided physical nourishment and friendliness during the countless hours I spent there as this was unfolding. Many important messages were received there—in particular, the teaching on Patience, which was a lesson in itself in the midst of much activity.

And to the many authors who have touched my life during this period, I feel so much gratitude. I could not mention them all in my book—I wish I could. In his or her own way, each has contributed to this process and I have been blessed by all of them. One I really need to single out is Ruth Montgomery for the incredible knowledge she has given us for decades and her willingness to "listen" and pass on the information she has received. The evidence of her risk-taking gives me strength.

And last, but by no means least, I wish to thank my husband, Dr. John Porter—physician and scientist. He didn't ask for this in his life. He didn't particularly welcome it. Some of this directly conflicts with his deeply held religious and scientific views. I wish to thank him for his patience, his tolerance, and his willingness to finally "go with the flow." I appreciate his sacrifice and love him dearly.

The
Story

A few years ago, I probably wouldn't have read a book like this. It wouldn't have appealed to me. I would have rejected it as unbelievable without even giving it, or me, a chance.

I was a skeptic, some would say an agnostic. Sure, I have been a life-long churchgoer (except for a brief few years in my early adulthood) and have always tried to live a moral life, a life of integrity. But I was hung up on the fear-based teachings of God in my past. I couldn't get past that. I couldn't reconcile a God of Love with a God of Wrath. To me, they did not, could not, go together. I couldn't accept the predominant version of sin. I couldn't accept an ideology that places the blame for all of the pain and suffering of the world—on the shoulders of a woman—a "disobedient" woman. So, in essence, I pushed all of that aside along with almost anything else about God. I just wouldn't deal with it. I would lead the life of a secular humanist while being active in my local church. I did good works; I even attended an adult Sunday School class. Somehow, I managed to stay uninvolved in the teachings that I refused to hear. Frankly, I ignored the whole concept of God. I truly didn't know if God existed, and I didn't see much evidence, if any, of God being a part of my everyday life.

Well, I was wrong—and my awakening—my spiritual awakening to God, came with a bang, accompanied by fireworks and lightshows.

In the fullness of its time my awakening came about, and even though it was cataclysmic, it has been so very gentle and filled with much love.

For that's what God is, you know. To me—God is Love. And fear-based teachings did not work for me, because deep down inside I had always known they were not correct for me. They are not a part of my path.

The catalyst for this awakening was the unheralded entrance into, and the subsequent exit from my life by death, of a young man who became very dear to me. At the moment of our meeting, I knew that he would be significant in my life. I never dreamed of the direction my life would take or the journey with God that would ensue.

His name was Kevin, and he was living in a half-way house located on the third floor of my church—what is known as "The Upper Room." My church is known for its local mission work. I have volunteered in its soup kitchen weekly for almost ten years.

Kevin became a very special part of my life and also the lives of some of my closest friends. In spite of terrible tragedies, years of manic depression, seizures, drug and alcohol abuse, and surviving a coma the previous year, there was something so innocent about him. Through it all, he had managed to hold on to an optimism that is not found in most people. God had shown me his spirit— and it was beautiful and glowing. You never know whom God will put in your midst. Please be open and willing to "see" with your heart.

Kevin needed much help, including doctors' visits, meetings with lawyers, support during court appearances, and meetings with probation officers and social service workers.

He had a dream—a dream of getting better and becoming a professional cook or even helping run a bed and breakfast. He had an incredible talent for cooking and was an accomplished artist. Before the coma, he created stunning works of art.

Kevin was a gentle, caring soul who had a tendency to put others before himself, often at his own expense. He had a chivalrous attitude toward women. Injustice bothered him deeply.

On his good days, we had profound discussions of philosophy and spirituality. Often he would tell me that he should have died many times, wondering why he was alive, wondering what use God still had for him.

Well, I honor him for what he brought to my life— inspiring changes I couldn't have imagined. He was in my life for only ten months. His health became progressively worse, and he died without warning on February 6, 1999, of an apparent heart attack. Kevin was thirty-one years old. My best friend and I discovered his body. It was one of the worst days of my life—filled with much heartache. Little did I know that I had been helping him tie up the loose ends of his life in preparation for death.

The day before his death, I had told God that Kevin was in God's hands. And then he died. I never questioned the rightness of what happened. I knew that Kevin's life had served its purpose—that his mission, his learning experiences on Earth, had been fulfilled. My knowledge of that did little to lessen the grief that we all feel when someone we care about dies. The knowledge that he was better off did not mean that I missed him any less, nor lessen the sadness I felt at the way his life had gone—a true child of God.

So how did a woman like me get to such a reliance on the will of God? During the time I knew Kevin, I became aware of God's guidance in my life. It was like I knew instinctively what I was to do for him. I just seemed to <u>know</u>. My actions didn't always make sense, certainly not to everyone around me, but they <u>felt</u> right. I learned to "listen" to my feelings. But I believe I'm also logical and reasonable, so I learned to balance the two—feelings and reason. That balance has continued on my journey.

His death was not the end of the journey—but the beginning of a most active phase.

On the day that my friend and I found his body, while I was still basically in shock, we were informed by our minister (at the time) that Kevin could not be given a Christian funeral. We were stunned. Turning down the minister's offer of a non-Christian funeral, I resolved to find someone else to officiate. God was working there, also. My husband reminded me of an acquaintance of ours, someone we had just recently spent time with at an anniversary celebration, who is an Episcopal priest. He was the perfect choice. During his years of attending Howe Military School, Kevin spent much time with an Episcopal priest there. I believe he was an altar boy. He spoke highly of the priest and shared wonderful stories of their times together. He had a beautiful silver crucifix hanging on the wall of his apartment that had been given to him by this special priest. I am proud and privileged to have that crucifix hanging on my wall in the room where most of this book came into being.

When we were going through Kevin's things after his death and I was on my way out the door, I was "guided" to look under the sofa cushions. The feeling just came upon me. There I found a small metal cross with the words "GOD LOVES YOU" on it, along with a dove. I remembered Kevin telling me that he always took it with him wherever he went and placed it underneath where he slept. I have kept it in my pocket ever since. It reminds me of Kevin, and it reminds me of God's love. It also reminds me of my connection to Jesus the Christ—a reminder that has been important to me during my spiritual journey.

Of course, this was a human being who did not deserve a Christian funeral. I think it must have been in that moment, when I was told that, that I made a decision. To me, those sentiments were not representative of God or of the teachings of Jesus the Christ. If those beliefs were correct, I felt I had nothing to lose. If they were incorrect, I had everything to gain. I resolved to throw out all of the religious teachings of my past and go on a search for God, myself. I had had incredible and loving experiences with God in the past year. That's why there was no fear in my undertaking. I thought I was embarking on a journey <u>to</u> God. I was actually traveling <u>with</u> God—on a journey that I believe was destined all along. Deep in my soul—I knew what I would find. And the treasure that I have uncovered is beyond anything I could ever have imagined.

I asked God to guide me on my journey. And I received such astounding guidance. To me, books and words are magic, so it is no wonder that many of the guideposts along my way have been books. I could just stand in front of the bookshelves in the bookstore and know what I was to read next. Before Kevin's death, I had begun to read books on spirituality, trying to find out what was going on with me. I was not familiar with the concept of "spiritual awakening." I had certainly never been exposed to what some people refer to as "New Age Spirituality." All of a sudden, it was as if I was famished for spiritual knowledge. But the knowledge I needed could not be found in traditional dogmas. So I read and read. In the last two years, I have read well over one hundred books on spirituality, and segments from others—from ancient to new age, Christian to Taoist to Wiccan. I gleaned whatever I needed from each one. Sometimes I needed almost everything in the book, other times I needed very little from it, but I always received whatever knowledge I needed at the time. It seemed like whatever was my most pressing question at the time was answered—just as James Redfield asserts in *The Celestine Prophecy* and his other books.

Sometimes I could just open a book, and the answer was right there on the page in front of me. Answers and Divine messages were everywhere. I learned to tune in to everything—overheard conversations, songs, signs, even license plates. Actually, license plates became a very important means of communication to me. Mystical experiences became more and more common in my life. Synchronicities abounded. The more open I became, the more guidance I received. I was a seeker looking for the truth—for what some call the unknowable—but I was being given answers. I developed an understanding and a sense of knowing that I had never experienced before.

Life had turned into an unexpected adventure! I was remembering God and loving almost every moment of it. I say almost, because it all seemed so unbelievable. I had been told that these things were impossible, but yet they were happening to me. I was experiencing them. Doubts and fear occasionally crept in. I usually managed to keep them at bay. I believe that a healthy dose of skepticism is important. One should think logically and reasonably and question. And that is what I did. I questioned, I tested, and I pondered. My reason told me that what I was experiencing was real—in an unreal sort of way. So the next question was, if this guidance was real, was it correct? It certainly seemed to be, but there were many things I couldn't prove. That's where faith comes in. Just because something can't be proven to exist, does not disprove its existence. My reading helped as I became aware that many other people were having mystical experiences similar to mine. I was not alone. There was validation in that. Even though each of us has our own unique experiences, there are similar mediums through which they occur.

Through it all, in what seems like a whirlwind to me now, my feeling of connection to God grew and grew. As someone who didn't see God working in my life before, I now saw the hand of God in everything. I, who did not pray much before, began speaking to God, talking out loud throughout the day. I learned I <u>could</u> trust the guidance. There was no reason for me to be misled. I had no ulterior motives. I just wanted truth and understanding.

Soon after Kevin died, I was led to a book group that was forming at Barnes and Noble—Spirituality Readers. Those gatherings fed my soul and brought three very special people into my life. Eventually, the four of us began meeting at other times to share our spiritual meanderings. Some of our interests were similar, some were different, but we discussed it all. No topic was out of bounds, and there has always been such a sense of respect for whatever anyone brought to the table. I believe that we have all stretched and grown through our times together. I certainly know I have.

Not long after I began my spiritual journey in earnest, I came across a book that was very meaningful to me. It was *In God's Truth* by Nick Bunick. That and another book about his story, *The Messengers,* brought the knowledge about angels into my life. Angels in today's world—not just in Biblical stories—affecting real people's lives. What an incredible story he had to tell, what an incredible mission he had to fulfill, what courage it took to come forward! He spoke about the number 444. How the angels use that number to remind us of the power of God's love. I began to see 444's all over the place at times that indicated significance, not just random chance. I realized that there had been significant connections with 444's indicated earlier in my journey, especially pertaining to Kevin, that I would never have realized without reading this book. I began to wonder if angels were somehow involved in giving me guidance and direction in my life. I had never believed in angels before, but this time it felt different. I was willing to consider the possibility that just maybe there are guardian angels, and maybe I was in a relationship with them. I couldn't see them, but I sure began to feel them. And indications of them were popping up all over the place, not just in 444's but in words, pictures, and representations. It was as if my consciousness was beginning to recognize their importance in my life.

I continued reading—books by psychics, books on reincarnation, and books that were channeled. My favorites were of people's personal experiences. I also read fiction that contained spiritual truths, scholarly books, and what some would consider really far-out books. All had something to give to me. I continued to grow and learn. There are so many incredible books out there whether you call them spiritual, metaphysical, or new age. I would consider reading anything as long as it came from the light. I wouldn't read anything that felt dark to me. That's not what my lessons were about. Most of the books I read would be called unconventional. As a friend says, I wouldn't listen to information coming to me in conventional ways. And she's absolutely right. I had tried that. It didn't work for me. But this was working for me. I had such a passion for the quest. God had become so real for me—so much a part of everything in my life. I was thriving.

I had everything in my life that most people think creates happiness, but there had been something indefinable missing. At last I knew what it was. It was my spiritual life—my connection to God. When you are aware of this connection, everything looks different. Events have so much meaning—they no longer seem random. Experiences become such opportunities for growth.

Months before, I had begun seeing a psychologist. I needed to make sense of the "strange" things that were happening in my life. To have someone to talk to who doesn't have an agenda has been extremely beneficial for me. The chance to unburden myself, to peel away the layers to my core, my Self, to be assured of my sanity in light of the unconventional things that were happening, is one of the most valuable gifts I have ever given myself. There is nothing to be ashamed of in this. This is a wise move and shows that you care about yourself, your real self. Her belief in me and her ability to discern and understand my spiritual journey has been a Godsend in my life, and I am very blessed to be working with her. God truly puts the right people in our lives at the right time. Try to accept this and embrace it.

But the angels had just begun with me. In August 1999, Doreen Virtue's book *Divine Guidance* came into my life. Here was someone who actually received messages from angels—she actually saw them! This raised my consciousness higher, yet again. More food for thought. I considered the possibilities. Then my daughter-in-law, Colleen, told me that Doreen was giving a workshop nearby. I couldn't believe it! I was not really into workshops but knew we needed to do this one. So we did. It was an amazing day! Doreen knew things that seemed impossible to know, yet she did. She opened my eyes to the possibilities of people actually working and healing with angels. I was enthralled. It felt so right to me. I began to believe that some gifted people could do this. It never occurred to me that I might be one of them.

Fast forward to March 2000. My husband, John, a physician, couldn't get free for Spring Break, so I decided to take my two sons and daughter-in-law on a vacation. My oldest son, Mathew, and his wife, Colleen, had been into "New Age" Spirituality for some time, certainly before I began my spiritual journey. They were having amazing experiences also, but that is their story to tell. We needed to decide where to go. I don't remember how we chose, but we decided to go to Sedona, Arizona. None of us had been there before, but we decided that Sedona would be the perfect place. It was. I had some unanswered questions that were puzzling me. I had considered going to a psychic, but that just didn't feel right. I had never been to a psychic before, and had never had any interest in doing so. Obviously, I needed answers—and the perfect person to help me was in Sedona. In the airport restroom, I overheard two ladies speaking about a town in Florida named Destiny. When I heard that, I thought, "Does this trip have to do with my destiny?" It most certainly did. The first day, I walked into a metaphysical store, and a woman asked me if I wanted a reading. If I had had time to think, I don't know if I would have had the courage to do it, but the timing was perfect. At that time, I did a thirty minute session. I went back later in the week for another hour. The reader's name is Shelia Schumate, and she is an Angelic Light Worker. Do you see the pattern here? A regular psychic was not right for me. I was sent all the way to Sedona to meet this particular Angelic Worker. She is such a beautiful person—you can feel the goodness surrounding her. She helped me with everything I needed to know at that time, drawing in guidance from my angels, guides, and my own higher self. The readings helped me immeasurably. But perhaps most important was the pattern of angels in my life giving me guidance.

I became aware of the guidance of my angels, even as they helped me with seemingly mundane things in my life, but which marred my serenity. Everyone jokes about the parking angels, but I always seem to find the right parking place. They have helped me find a dress for a special event and a winter coat when it had turned very cold and I had little time to shop. How do I know they helped? I could feel them. I knew exactly where to park, which store to go to, even which rack my dress or coat would be hanging on. You may find all of this ridiculous, but it is impossible for me to describe the experience, the sense of knowing that I get when they help me, when they lead me to something specific. What this did for me was to make me aware of the angels and guides in my life—to be open to the next step—the bigger picture—much bigger than finding a dress or a coat.

My birthday is July 13th. I was born on Friday the 13th—the day sacred to the Goddess. This has played a part in the unfolding of my destiny also. Last year on my birthday, I received an extra-special gift. Someone close to me gave me a message from God with a book to accompany it. I have a friend who has heard the voice of God for as long as she can remember. On occasion, she receives messages for other people. This was my blessed day. Here is the message: "Blessed you are, Linda, with the gift of words—the flow on paper—and the eyes to see the beauty of words and their magic written by others. Now it is time, God has told me—for you to begin your journey of words—He will guide you—just let it flow however it does—and trust Him—(God)." Upon opening the other gift, I was stunned. I had such a "gut reaction" to it. I knew it was absolutely right. The book is *The Right to Write–An Invitation and Initiation into the Writing Life* by Julia Cameron. I had been told—guided—but I still wasn't ready. There was too much fear left in me. Me, write? I found it hard to believe. Yes, books are a passion of mine, but I like to read other people's words. What could I possibly have to say?

Later that same month, more prodding came my way. I "accidentally" stumbled upon the *Angelspeake* series of books by Barbara Mark and Trudy Griswold. With the first one I was spellbound. I quickly read the next two. These are books about talking to and working with your personal angels. I knew of those who went into a trance to let spirits speak through them or messages that somehow were written without the human writer knowing what they contained—and I was petrified. No way, I thought, would I turn myself over to that! But these books talked about angel dictation. Maybe I would be willing to do that, but I certainly didn't have the ability to do it. And besides, I was too frightened to even try. Ask the angels a question and see what comes? You've got to be kidding. They weren't kidding.

This brings us to September. I decided it was time to work with the writing book I had been given. This book was, in essence, about creative writing in a spiritual way. Good choice. Julia Cameron talks about doing morning pages—writing three pages every morning about anything that comes. Don't direct it. Just see what comes. So I began. I loved it! Sometimes very profound things showed up, and sometimes I just rambled. I was learning so much about myself in the process. But on a day in mid-September, everything changed. I was in the habit in my journaling of asking questions. On that day, I received a response that I immediately realized did not come from me. Well, it came through me, but not from me. Rather hard to explain. Once again, I was stunned! I am a rational person, and I didn't expect anything like this! It was as if they had decided that if I wouldn't come to them, they would come to me. Here's what I wrote in my journal on September 15, 2000: "Help me to take this love and use it to shine light and love on others. Please." Here was the response:

> *It will be done. It is done everyday. You can't imagine. But trust that it is done. You have so much beauty and light and love to give. People are aware of it. That's what they're seeing, sensing, and appreciating. You shine. You positively glow. Shine on and be grateful for what you have been given. Amen.*

Excuse me? I wondered where in the world this came from. Actually, it didn't come from this world at all. I wondered if I could possibly, accidentally, have made it up. But I knew that there was no way I would have said such nice things about myself. No way.

In the beginning, I received a message every few days. Then they started coming more often. They were fairly short at first and with time became longer and longer. I assume that my abilities were getting stronger. After awhile, I no longer needed the morning pages to receive their messages. I began to "feel" when one was coming. Sometimes they come when I'm driving or at other inopportune moments, like the night I was at the Symphony.

In those cases, I ask them to wait until I have an opportunity to write the messages. They respect my wishes,
but sometimes I know they want me to hurry. I've been
known to pull into a parking lot unexpectedly. And I've
learned to always carry paper and pen with me.

The following are some of the early messages that I
feel offer some important information as to this process:

09/21/00

"Angels, what would you have me do to facilitate better
communication with us, if anything?"

> *Just let it flow. Be comfortable with it. We
> will come to you when needed. Relax.
> Don't worry—we'll be back.*

I did worry. What if that was it? What if I'd had these
amazing experiences and then they were all over? Oh, ye
of little faith.

09/29/00

"That makes me wonder about how do I know when the
messages are real or whether I'm interpreting them correctly?"

> *You know messages are real. The timing is
> not always the same as you expect. There
> are always reasons behind something that
> you can't understand. Don't doubt the
> messages. Just accept them and move on.
> Wait for the explanation to come. It will
> and then you will understand. You are be-
> ing led and you know that. Remember to
> trust and follow the guidance. We won't
> let you down.*

10/01/00

"Will I ever get comfortable with this?"

> *Just keep trying. You will be more comfortable in time. Let the words flow. Don't try to stop them or create them. They come when they come.*

They continued writing me beautiful messages and giving me guidance. And occasionally I would be given messages for others. The first one was hard to deliver and they still are to this day. And then I received the message telling me who they are:

10/18/00

> *. . . Your higher self is important too and you get much wisdom from within. But we are your guides and teachers and as such love you and support you. We are here to protect you and guide you along your path. You are to teach others about us. Everyone needs to know of this support. This will be beneficial to them.*

Later that evening marked a turning point in my life. I received a phone call from a young woman who is very special to me. She called to tell me that she was in the hospital, about to have her baby at 27 weeks. She asked me to pray for her and her baby. I was so worried. That was very early for the baby to be born. I was touched that she wanted me to pray for her. It was only a short time before that I had become comfortable praying for someone else. I was guided to that by a special friend, Ike, from my church, who was really into prayer and knew it was time for me to take that step. Praying for yourself is one thing, but taking the responsibility for someone else was very daunting until I realized that I need only pray for someone's highest good and for healing in whatever way is best, and for them to be given the strength and courage to get through the ordeal in the best way possible. God's will be done.

I was so happy to pray for her and her baby. Soon after I finished praying, a message began coming. I discounted it, thinking I was making it up. It came again, so I wrote it down. It was a beautiful message to my friend. I do not reveal other people's messages to anyone else, as I believe that they are personal from God and the angels. But my friend has given me permission to share this one:

> *Your baby will be fine. Yes, she is coming early but time will take care of everything. Please do not worry. Just shower her with love. Everything will be fine.*

"Did I get your message correctly?"

> *Yes, everything will be fine. You'll see. This will prove to you that we're right. You can trust us, as we know you do. It is right for you to question at this point. We understand. But you will see that we're correct. Everything will be fine.*

"Is the baby a girl?"

> *Yes, absolutely.*

"I am right about all of this, aren't I?"

> *Yes, you are. You know. You believe. You trust us. We have a long way to go together and many wonderful things to do. Many people will be helped. Love, it's about love. You are helping us to share and spread the*

love of God. We have chosen a worthy
partner for this endeavor. You're right. Your
life will change. It will only get better. The
trust you have shown us makes us joyous.
We have chosen well. Do not be afraid. All
is going well. We love you and will talk to
you later.

I knew that this was a defining moment in my life. I had been given information about the future—verifiable information. If the information was wrong, I would have to begin again, but where to start? If the information was correct, my life would truly change, big-time. But first I had to wait. I opted not to tell anyone. I needed to learn this lesson on my own. The night seemed very long. Finally, in the morning, I found out. My friend had a little girl that weighed less than three pounds. But she was doing really well. She spent weeks in the hospital but progressed wonderfully. She is now thriving. What a blessing for them and also for me.

My journey continued. I tried not to let this overwhelm me. It was so hard to believe, but yet it was happening. My biggest fear was that somehow I was making this up and would mislead others. What if I told them something that was not true? I couldn't bear the thought, because truth is so important to me. Even though I knew I couldn't be making this up, the fears did creep in occasionally. My youngest son, Alex, said, "No offense Mom, but there is no way you could make this up." I look back now and see this as a necessary part of the process. And doubts still creep in occasionally, but not as often, and they are more easily dismissed.

I continued getting messages, usually on a daily basis, sometimes more than once a day. Then in early

November, I started receiving much longer messages—pages at a time. It seemed as though I was being prepared for something new. I had no idea of the magnitude of the next lesson they had planned for me. It's a good thing!

On November 4, 2000, I received the following message:

We're proud of you. Your trust in us, all of us, is gratifying to us. You will get through all of this with bells on. You have so much in store for you. Keep calm and feel the love. You know of the love that surrounds you. Don't be afraid to believe. It's all here. The work continues and will be picking up speed. Is that possible, you ask? Yes, it certainly is. Be prepared, but be calm. All can be handled well by you. We are so proud of you, Precious One. We love you inordinately. Go with PEACE. Have a good day, Precious. Love.

"Thank you so much. Did this message come from you?"

Yes, it did. We are always so happy to talk to you. You are a bright spot to us. We love you. Just remember that. We expect big things from you and you will handle them with ease. You are so attuned to the mission. Even though you don't know the specifics, you are willing to trust us, to trust God, and to follow where you are led. We'll end for now. Remember we love you.

From the beginning of my communications with them, I had felt so surrounded by love. They were so affirming and provided so much support and encouragement. There is no way that I can describe the love that is given by them. And this love would certainly be needed for the next big step.

It was the morning of November 7th, Election Day. I said a prayer, asking that the winner be the right person to lead this country. I felt that this was a very important election. Before I went to vote, I settled down to receive my message for the day. Finishing that, and assuming that we were done, I started to put my pen down. To my surprise, another message began forming. I was stunned again! My angels seem to produce that effect in me a lot.

The election will be fine. George Bush will win as he is right to lead this country. He is a man of God and feels love for all. He will be a great leader—bring people together. This country is in for a surprise. You were right that talk of hatred, evil, and fear and divisiveness can not prevail. The people will see this. This man has a beautiful spirit and it will show across the land and the planet. He is the first big step—a truly spiritual leader. One that will lead and spread hope and love across this country. His wife will be a beautiful asset. You will connect with this man as you have already. You sense the beauty of his spirit. Things will not be as close as predicted—you'll see. We're putting ourselves on the line for you—to convince you. Do not be afraid. We're correct. You know that. Go with love, Little One. No, you did not ask for proof. This is not a game to you. This is serious and sacred and your attitude and reverence is what makes you so blessed. You are such a good woman. Believe it. Don't forget to vote. Every vote counts.

No, I had not asked for this. I didn't even want it. Being told things in advance and then waiting for the outcome is extremely difficult for me—certainly lessons in patience, worry, and trust. But of course, I would know the outcome that night, or so I thought. As to the timing, I was very wrong—by more than a month—with much anguish. It's a good thing I didn't know that then.

By the next morning I did not view this as a gift! We still didn't know who the President would be. But, during the unfolding of what seemed like chaos, I received many messages, at least twenty, telling me that George Bush would be the winner. I will share some of them with you.

But first, a word about my connection with President Bush. I have been a life-long Democrat, my husband, John, a life-long Republican—although, I tend to vote for the person. And frankly, I was disgusted with what seemed to me to be the lack of character and integrity in the Clinton Administration.

John became a big supporter of George W. Bush. I couldn't understand that. We hadn't even had the primaries. We had no clue as to what he stood for, what his ideology of government was. I didn't think I could ever support him.

All of that changed early in the Summer. I turned on the television. George W. Bush was speaking in Tennessee. It was a beautiful speech—about loving your neighbor. He mentioned synagogues and mosques along with churches. He said that we needed a new spirit of love in this country. His words truly brought tears to my eyes. It was as if in that moment, God allowed me to "see" his spirit and it was beautiful. It was an amazing experience! After that, I began watching and listening to him. The more I saw, the more I became convinced that he was for real—that he was truly a caring and compassionate man, a godly man, and accepting of all faiths. To me, he did not seem at all to be the way he was being portrayed by his detractors. Then, shortly before the election, I heard it said that this election was about good versus evil, implying that George Bush was evil. Truthfully, that disgusted me. I felt that talk like that and other divisive rhetoric that was being used could not be good for this country. When would we have healing? How could we live up to the promise that our founders envisioned?

At the soup kitchen where I work, I haven't seen hope in the eyes of the people who eat there, I've seen resignation. Well, I want something better for those people—for everyone. There will always be those among us who need help. And along with the material help, they should be valued as the children of God that they are, and receive love. Love gives hope. Love and hope can sometimes work miracles.

So on Election Day, even though I was supporting Governor Bush, I had no idea how this would all unfold, or what role the presidential election would play in my future. And what seemed so big at the time was all part of a much bigger picture—leading me to write this book and presenting the angels' incredible and beautiful teachings to the world. That Election Day message and subsequent ones established my credibility with many. And many of my family and friends who were supporters of Al Gore were not at all happy with me. They had mixed feelings. In this case, they wanted me to be wrong. There was some tension involved. I was very careful who I told, but I was guided in who I should tell and also who to share my messages with, so I did, sometimes with much trepidation.

This was a very difficult period for me. After all, I was having to learn how to trust them myself. What would I do if the information was wrong? I felt like my future was at stake here, and it basically was. I knew that the angels would not intentionally mislead me, but I truly needed to learn this by experience. And I didn't really see how George Bush could pull this out, but yet I knew he would. The angels told me so, repeatedly. At this time, I would like to share some excerpts from their very prophetic and encouraging messages. And even though I am intuitive, I do not consider myself to be a psychic. I am given the information by my angels and guides. It's that simple. Simple, huh?

11/09/00

> *Please do not worry, Little One. All will be fine. The waiting is hard. We know. You are doing well to put it aside for awhile. The outcome is determined. So you sit and wait. You feel your future is on the line here. But what better hands to be in—God's hands and our guidance. God is in control.*

11/10/00

> *We're proud of you. You've shown such strength today. That took such courage for*

you to put this out there. You needed to do that for various reasons that will all become clearer at a later date. You trust us and also know that it is time for you to determine the truth. Are we real? You know we are. But you need to find out for sure. We understand your doubt. We expect it. That is all part of the process. We have come a long way in a short time. To you, it seems. We have been guiding you all along, you just weren't aware of it. The time was right for you to awaken. And awaken you have! We couldn't be more pleased. You are looking forward to the future of this country. As well you should. You will have played a part, you know. The importance of it will be revealed later. George Bush will win, you know. It is God's will. Much depends on this. He has been being prepared for years. The love and compassion for his fellow man is real. He knows he is to fulfill this role for God. That's why he is steadfast in his belief that he will win. Yes, it is hard for him but he will be able to bring the country together. You don't see how, but it will happen. Trust us. It will be a glorious time.

11/11/00

Free will does enter in, but this decision is so important to the future of mankind that there are no areas of chance in this. George W. Bush will be President. We assure you the outcome will be as desired—not just

*by you, but by the designs of God, the Cre-
ator. We would not tell you something that
is not certain. It would serve no purpose.
And we have much to do—for the Glory
of God.*

11/12/00

*This will all be over soon. Of course, you
know how we are with time. Things are
happening as we speak. Behind the scenes.
The country will be dismayed by all of this,
but eventually it will be over and things
will go smoothly—as smooth as it ever is
in Washington!*

11/13/00

*George W. Bush will be President of the
United States. He will do a wonderful job
leading this country. The country will be
brought together, healed of many ills. Keep
your faith about it. Do not let anyone cause
you doubts.*

11/16/00

*Still your mind, Little One. You know the
answer, the outcome. All of these setbacks,
that aren't really setbacks—just hurdles
that can be, that will be crossed. The process continues, but the outcome will be the
same. George W. Bush will be President of
the United States. Governor Bush will have
a mandate—maybe not in traditional thinking, but nonetheless. What is a mandate?
It means that the majority of the people*

will accept him soon. They may not all be happy about it, but they will accept the results. Incredible things will happen in this country. Believe us. You will be a part of it—in your way. We are pleased that you have accepted the challenge—a call to arms. Not of violence, but with peace and love— arms across to each other, around each other in love. This will all begin soon. Be prepared.

11/19/00

There is no more room for old thinking. Time to move on—to a better world—a better way of thinking. We assure you, George Bush will become President. It will be announced soon. No matter—the outcome will be the same. This is bad and disruptive, but in the end, all will come out okay. You know that.

11/21/00

Everything is okay. If Al Gore were to win, would this not all be over? Things are being worked out. George Bush will win. You have been allowed to know things that others don't. You know the importance of this election. God will prevail. It is written in time. George W. Bush will be President— will be declared soon. You have seen so much. But so many others on both sides have been blind. The blindness is worse than you thought, is it not? But God is in control. And it is time for humans to evolve further. You are a part of that. Look at you! How far you've come in a short time. And you will help with others. It is decreed. You can touch many lives—and help people to understand George W. Bush and his importance. Things must be looked at in different ways. Throw out the old and begin again—at the beginning.

11/24/00

All is well. Things are winding down. It will be over soon. George W. Bush will be declared the winner soon. Be prepared to spread the message. The (original) message and others and tell how they came about. Remember—do not worry about skeptics. You know what you know. You don't have to prove yourself or us to others. Just put out the information and let people do what they will. Do not become defensive and do not worry. Some will believe in you—some won't. That is no reflection on you. Obviously, though, you have been chosen for this because of your believability and your grace.

11/25/00

You see everything possible being done to stop George Bush's Presidency. It is all in vain. He will become President. However it will happen, it will happen. Have faith. Things are happening all over the place. You know who the winner will be. Then you will do what you need to do.

Later:

Whatever is done to hamper this will be met with resistance. There is no way that George Bush will lose. Supreme efforts are being made at this time—ongoing efforts to assure the outcome. There are many surprises—ongoing. That is why we told you it is the results, not the process that counts in this case. This will all come out correctly—George Bush will win. This battle amazes even us. There is so much selfishness in the world. So much effort to win— at any cost. Things must change and will.

11/27/00 (following the declaration)

Congratulations, you have a winner! A long time coming, but here all the same. The rest is just unimportant. George W. Bush is the winner—he will become the President of the United States on January 20, 2001. You will be elated. The country will settle down and all will go well. Take time now to just relax. You'll know what to do next.

12/01/00

All will go well. It will take time, but George W. Bush will prove himself. There will always be those that are unhappy and criticize but the majority will be fine. Tempers are stirred up, no doubt about that. They will take time to still. It is unfortunate that it went this way. Choices are made. Either path taken, the destination,

the outcome is the same. Miracles do hap-
pen you know. You will be part of many.
You recognize them—from small to large.
Have faith. Faith is needed here—regard-
ing the outcome of the election.

12/04/00

Things are unfolding as we said, are they
not? It will be over soon. You have shown
faith and trust in spite of the unsettling
things that have been going on. We salute
you. You will need strength in light of skep-
ticism. But you know that. You've seen
miracles in action. You've been privileged
to be a part of this unfolding, as have those
around you. Yes, it has been hard but you
have survived quite well—still continuing
to share your love and light with others.
You will have the courage to share the mes-
sages and you will know who to share with.
Do not take any responses personally. Some
definitely will not want to hear this mes-
sage. But others will revel in it. Be open to
all. Do not discriminate. Put the informa-
tion out there—then stand back. Be avail-
able but not pushy. They will seek you
out—the ones that want to know more. Do
not be dissuaded by negative reactions—
and there will be some. You know that. But
you are strong and beautiful and have
God's guidance on your side. Again, be
prepared for skepticism, but don't take it
personally. You know what you know. You
are filled with love and joy. It will be beau-

tiful. Some things will take time, but others will happen quickly. George Bush will win many over quickly. They will see, as you have seen. Many are blinded. They have lived with untruth for so long, it's hard to recognize the truth. But eventually, many will see.

12/06/00

You need to spread the message about the election and about the beauty of George Bush's spirit. You will do it in the right way. Do not be too humble or modest. Be matter of fact—you did receive the message. You were chosen for that. Do not lessen the gift you have been given. But also do not allow it to become an ego thing. You will get the proper balance—no falseness about you. Facts are facts, and with love and caring, and a willingness to serve, it will come out just right. We are not saying to never be humble—just that a balance is needed for the message to be its most effective. You can do this. You will do this. It is your way.

12/07/00

All will be fine. It will be over soon. George Bush will be the President. Steps must be taken to heal this divisiveness. Miracles do happen. You know that. You believe. This looks like another setback. It will all work out. We heard your plea for strength and courage. You have much. There is no rea-

son for you to be misled. We assure you—
George W. Bush will win. Free will is an
amazing thing, is it not? But destiny wins
out—one way or another. There are many
prayers being said. You'd be amazed how
many are being said for you. We will move
past this—eventually—and you will have
much to say. Hang on a little while longer.
You are used to miracles, are you not? More
on the way. Be assured.

12/11/00

Do not be afraid. You will know what to
do when the time is right. You are right to
worry—no not worry, but wonder how
people will respond to your message of
hope about the election of George W. Bush
as President. The country is divided right
now, but many will get over it. That is
where you come in. You must help with
the healing. We will show you what to do.
You can do it easily. Again, you will put
the information out there. People will have
the freedom to choose whether to believe
or not. That is their prerogative. Many will
choose to believe in spite of themselves.
Time—it will take time. You will be able
to "pull this off"—your words. We could
say—"This will reach a successful conclusion." Have no fear today. Believe. All will
go according to plan. What will you say
about miracles? You've seen many, have
you not? Be strong under fire. There will
be some, you know. Remain calm and as-

sured. You know what you know. Serenity is needed. Don't allow the freedoms of others to frustrate you. You have seen so much. You know how God works. With God, anything is possible. You do know that. Tell people of God's will. It is important. But don't allow the skepticism to affect you.

Well, as we all know by now, George W. Bush did become President of the United States on January 20, 2001. I had the privilege and the honor to be at the Inauguration and the festivities that followed. I can not begin to describe my feelings on that day. To me, this was about so much more than politics. I truly believe in this man. How can I not? God has shown me his spirit, and the angels have told me something of his mission. The Inauguration of George W. Bush as President of the United States was one of the most important days of my life. To me, it was a sacred day, and his speech was a sacred speech, filled with his love of and commitment to God, his love and compassion for his fellow men and women, his value of and commitment to a better life for all, and his dedication to this country and its ideals. And even I was surprised when in his speech he spoke these words, "an Angel rides in the whirlwind and directs this storm." When people ask me how I was able to go to the Inauguration, I tell them it was a gift from God paid for with my husband's Earthly money! It was certainly a fitting finale to that phase of my training and service. I couldn't help but wonder what would be coming next!

Since the beginning, I have received many incredible messages and teachings from my angels and guides. Their messages are uplifting, encouraging, loving, and supporting. Their guidance has always proven to be correct, even though the predicted outcome sometimes seems impossible, or at the very least, in doubt. They never dictate to me, tell me what to do, but they do make suggestions. The decision whether to follow or not is totally up to me. And they have assured me that it is fine to question and doubt. But they have been so accurate, my doubts occur less frequently. And it's not that I doubt them, it's myself I doubt. What if I made it up—what if I didn't translate their message correctly? I have learned to trust them and God. But this is not blind trust, it is based on experience. There are those who tell me this is impossible. It is not impossible; it happens to me. Why is it so much easier to believe that all of these experiences are random accidents, than that there is a loving, guiding hand involved? Let's get real here!

My angels and guides have become such trusted, loving friends to me. They have become as real as any physical beings in my life. No, I don't know their specific names at this time. They and I have agreed to use the name Us for the entire group. This is what makes me comfortable. And as they always say, it's the message that counts, not the messenger.

Not only do they give me written messages, but I carry on a dialogue with them in writing. I ask questions whenever I want. On 11/15/00, this was my question for them:

"Do I have different angels and guides for different kinds of help?"

> *Yes, we are specialists—except for your guardian angels from birth and loved ones. The ones that help you with spiritual messages—Bible verses, etc., are not the same ones that help you find clothes, etc. We call in whoever is needed at the time. They*

come and go—but your true lifetime guard-
ian angels stay with you constantly—keep-
ing you safe and giving you love—sur-
rounding you with love. They are constant
in your life. But we all love you—uncondi-
tionally.

And on 01/25/01, I asked: "Why am I getting so much help?"

Because you need it. Because you believe
it. We promised you we would help you
when you came to Earth—to the physical.
You have woken up to the spiritual realm.
You believe in us. You listen to your guid-
ance, you trust us. You are so loved and
cherished. Plus, also, this is important to
your path, your mission. You have so much
to do, to accomplish. You need to be con-
stantly aware of the support around you,
so you can help others. You are to make
others aware of us—not for excitement or
sensationalism, but to give them hope.
People have so much hope when they feel
loved. They must be made aware of God's
love for them. You have agreed to do this—
at whatever the cost to yourself. Therefore,
we are here for you—to help in whatever
way we can. You deserve love, support, and
help, and you can depend on it. So have
peace of mind today, Little One. We are
there for you. Always. Be grateful. We
know you are.

They have given me wonderful advice about my health

and about my decades long struggle with food and weight, and even whether it was safe to use a particular product on my face. They were right! They seem to know it all—or at least have the ability to find out. And it certainly seems sometimes that they anticipate my questions, which is not so surprising, is it? If you're going to believe in them at all, why not believe in this aspect of their abilities?

As I am writing this, they are telling me to remind you of their connection to God. Because that is where the help and the knowledge really comes from. I believe that some would refer to angelic help as coming from the Holy Spirit. There are many ways this is manifested. This just happens to be the particular way that works for me. And again, it all depends on your openness. Divine guidance is everywhere, available for everyone. Paul even talks about spiritual gifts in 1 Corinthians, Chapter 12, Verses 1-11. And I quote, beginning with verse 4: "There are different kinds of spiritual gifts but the same Spirit; there are different forms of service but the same Lord; there are different workings but the same God who produces all of them in everyone. To each individual the manifestation of the Spirit is given for some benefit. To one is given through the Spirit the expression of wisdom; to another the expression of knowledge according to the same Spirit; to another faith by the same Spirit; to another gifts of healing by the one Spirit; to another mighty deeds; to another prophecy; to another discernment of spirits; to another varieties of tongues, to another interpretation of tongues. But one and the same Spirit produces all of these, distributing them individually to each person as he wishes."

I feel so blessed with the spiritual gifts I have been given, and now they feel perfectly right for me. What seemed so abnormal at the beginning, feels so normal to me now. And I sometimes forget that others might find me and my way of living unconventional, perhaps even threatening. I can assure you there is nothing threatening about it. To be aware of the love of God surrounding you at all times is the greatest gift imaginable. And this gift is available for everyone. All you need to do is ask for it, be open to it, believe in it, recognize it, and accept it when it comes. I would encourage everyone to open up and tap into the form of Divine guidance that is waiting for you. Your angels and guides have waited a long time to help you in this way. Give them a chance. They do this for your benefit. And you will receive help undreamed of.

Now, you might be wondering how someone like me is found quoting Bible scripture. That was something else I pushed aside in my life—too threatening. And it can be, the way it is presented by some. To me, the Bible is full of much beauty and much wisdom, but it is also a historical document, containing many stories from a time much more violent than the time we live in. Humankind is continually evolving, and even though it doesn't always seem like it, we have come a long way from such a violent past. There is literature, poetry, and to me, much symbolism in the Bible. I have learned to read the Bible in the same way I read other books on spirituality. I listen to what speaks to me, and if it "feels" dark to me, I pass on it. Darkness is not a part of my path. And as for the New Testament, the teachings of Jesus the Christ are unsurpassed.

My angels and guides gave me a beautiful and wonderful message on 01/30/01 regarding the teachings of Jesus the Christ. This one is difficult for me to share, but I feel that it is of such importance that I humbly share it with you. Think what you will of it:

> *Look forward to Spring—the rebirth. And make a joyous event out of Easter. Christ has shown the way—Rebirth and Life Everlasting. What an incredible gift "He" gave to this world. Teachings of LOVE and CONNECTION to GOD. Learn from his teachings and remember his love for you. You are one of his chosen disciples. Do not be daunted by this. You can do it. You are much closer to him than you realize. You first must be released from the fear teachings of the past. You are working on it. Then you will be more able to share his teachings of love, divineness, ability to create, and our awesome connection to God— much greater than people used to realize. But you know this, have been taught this. Your teachers have taught you well, have they not? And much more to come. We are so pleased with your abilities, your willingness, and your hunger and thirst for our teachings. The Way of God is so awesome. You will teach that—in your own way. You will reach many. So, relax your worries and fears and trudge ahead. All will unfold as it should. Get out of its way—and allow it to happen.*

This was difficult to share because of the words, "one of his chosen disciples." I was stunned when I read it, and I was afraid that those of you reading it would think I was being presumptuous. How dare I? But then I decided to distance myself from my interpretation of the word disciple and look it up in the dictionary. The meaning given reassured me. Disciple—one who assists in spreading the teachings of another. To me, Jesus is a Master, and I am committed to doing my best to spread his teachings accurately. Isn't that what ministers, priests, and church lay people do? Mine is just in a different format. I don't profess to be accomplished at it yet, but I am committed to learning and sharing, and I certainly couldn't ask for better teachers! I will just have to trust them on this, and do my very best.

I have several friends who encouraged me to look at the Bible anew. One deserves special mention. Her name is Doris, and she works at the Soup Kitchen with me. She is a fine Christian woman and a true servant of God. I can not thank her enough for her belief in me and her support and encouragement. I remember the day she told me that God was preparing me for something. Neither she nor I could have imagined this! For more than two years, week after week, over pots of soup (she cooking and dipping, me putting on the lids and wiping the cups for carry-out), she has mentored me in Christian Spirituality. She patiently answered my questions and would provide whatever scripture I needed at the time. She always knew exactly what I needed to be given, whether it was what I wanted to hear or not. I have no doubt that God speaks through Doris. That is one of her spiritual gifts. I would go home and look up the scripture. Little by little, I learned not to be frightened of the words. And I also learned to interpret the words in the way they spoke to me. But what was amazing to me was how these teachings, in their own way, mirrored teachings found in other World Religions, even in New Age Spirituality. I began to see a pattern. The more I saw a pattern, the more I read the same teachings from vastly different sources, the more it appeared to me that these were Universal Truths. I have long believed that there is more than one path to God—that each person must find his or her own path, the one that resonates with each of them. I believe that my readings and my angelic messages substantiate this. Not everyone believes this. That is his or her choice. But I have found my path, and it is bliss. I remember Joseph Campbell urging us to follow our bliss. I have done just that. This is the way that works for me, and I bask in its warmth.

Recently, I had begun feeling that I should go through my notebooks and input all of my angelic writings onto the computer. I didn't want anything to happen to them. Others had told me that there could be a book made of them. I'm not sure I took that too seriously, although I have learned to listen and process anything that is said to me, and I have learned not to discount any possibility. I also knew that there was a Divine reason for my receiving these messages. This had to go beyond just helping me. There had to be a bigger picture. I have learned to be as patient as possible and let things unfold in their time. I also knew that I would be told what to do. Furthermore, I knew that I needed to save my writings and organize them by category to the best of my ability. Categorizing is somewhat difficult, because often several subjects are covered in one message. Soon after I began this process, I received this message:

01/27/01

> *Do not be ashamed to talk about us or share our messages. That is a part of your path. Again, we are not a sideshow routine, but a true and honest gift from God.*

One that people need to be made aware of. It is time. More and more people are being directly contacted to work with the Angels and proclaim the Divine Messages. You are one of them. One of many, you know that. There are many you are to enlighten and educate. You are perfect. We chose well—and you accepted this holy challenge. You have what it takes. Believe in yourself. We know you believe in us. Believe wholeheartedly in us. And spread the message. You know when and who to share with. More on the way. Be open to possibilities for sharing. But also be careful. Choose the right means and medium for doing so. Books are in your future, you know. You don't know how, but it will come to pass. But you are not ready yet. You need much more information. Continue being open to us—and we will give it to you. Stunning information! You think we are not modest but we know what we know. We too work for God and for the betterment of all. We will help you on your Earthly mission—to enlighten—as you help us with ours. We all learn and grow and love . . . Continue to share your love and light and your healing spirit with others. Show love, but be true to yourself, and your mission.

I hardly dared allow myself to consider what they had said. Books and the written word are my passion. How could I possibly consider producing a book of my own—and with angels no less!

Almost all of my messages had related to me, problems I was trying to solve, things I was trying to work through, information that I needed to make my daily life flow better. And they were filled with acceptance, love, support, and encouragement. Sometimes they told me something I didn't want to hear, didn't want to know. But these messages were always encased in love and provided the advice needed to work through them. Growth on Earth certainly does not always involve what appears to be entirely love and light. There are shadows and darkness to experience. As they reminded me on 01/27/01:

> *Life goes on. The shadows will lighten, the Sun will come out and another cycle will begin. Be prepared. Work through the shadows. There is even more growth ahead. Trudge ahead. You signed up for much growth in this lifetime. But sit back and let us help you. No, that is not being too dependent or shirking your responsibility. Besides, our guidance is not always easy for you, is it? Sometimes you long for peace. But you will find it—with us, with God. Good times are ahead for you—loving times, serene times.*

Growth often is not easy. But the love and light are always there and during the hard times we must not forget that, and we must remember to focus on hope. We were not sent to Earth to fend for ourselves, alone. There is help everywhere, even though you might not recognize it. We receive much help from those who share this physical space with us, but we also are surrounded with much help and support from the spiritual realm. All you need do is ask for it. That is the key. God has given us free will. Spiritual beings are not allowed to interfere with that. But they are ready and waiting, and so want to help you. They are a gift from God—evidence of God's great love for us. Do not continue to deny yourself this help. Realize your worth. You have a spark of the Divine in you. Don't you see how truly awesome that is—how truly awesome _you_ are? This help is yours for the asking. Accept it and be grateful.

Throughout the months leading to this point, I have been told of other parts of my mission. More than once I have received the words <u>TRUST</u>, <u>SERVE</u>, <u>LOVE</u>. I have been told this is my path. Here are some examples of the knowledge I have been given:

10/13/00
In response to: "This is such a blessing that I find it hard to believe that I deserve it."

> _It's not a matter of deserving, but one of serving. We trust you. We love you. We will help you in whatever way we can. You are deserving of our love. Go forth and serve. That is your path._

10/21/00

> _Be there to support, to nurture, to love. People will need to feel your loving kindness. That never goes out of style. Be available to love. That is your uniqueness. The love you share can not be duplicated. That is you._

10/29/00

"I still don't really understand what my mission—my 'work' is to be."

> *It is to provide love. People will look to you for love and understanding . . . You have learned so much of many different kinds of beliefs and views that you can bring an understanding to any circumstance. You bring in unconditional love. You always had that in you, but you were afraid. You had such a feeling of your own unworthiness. You couldn't get past that to others. But you always radiated kindness when you allowed yourself to connect with others. So many years you spent like that. But now you have come out of all of that. The love overflows. Fear has lessened drastically, as it should. Again, love. You will be expected to show love—something you have been well trained for—it comes naturally to you. You just need to let yourself "go" and it comes out. Your path concerns this. Do not be apprehensive. All is going well—extremely well. You can do this. And you are surrounded by love. You know this. Thank you for paying attention to the signs and accepting them. It makes our work easier. You are a treasure and we are well pleased. Go in love and continue loving.*

11/06/00

> *First, your work. It is love—to share and spread Love. Love comes from God. You*

possess it in abundance. We are so proud of you—to begin to show the love inside. That took courage. You are asked to share this love and caring. You are serene, usually, and bring a calming effect to people. . . . We will take care of you—with love and support unlike you could have dreamed of. Much more. We know how we feel with your love and trust. We hope we bring the same to you. Our love is always there for you. Reach for it. Reach for the stars! You will be amazed at what will happen and is happening to you.

11/12/00

. . . You know we have much to do—for God and for Love. One and the same, aren't they? Pure, loving, light. It is put through you to others . . . It's okay to be scared—expected even. But you move forward. Do not be afraid. Do not allow fear to take over . . . Be steadfast in your belief.

11/16/00

You can't help spreading light. It's in you— it is you. It comes directly from God and is a gift you have accepted, embraced with joy. You thought you weren't connected to people—but look at you. You touch almost everyone you meet . . . You have such a good and loving heart. It's time you took it out of the closet . . . There are some people it's hard to glow around. Be tolerant. Keep showing by example.

12/16/00

Do not be shy or ashamed of what you are doing. This is a wonderful gift you have been given and are passing along. We so applaud your willingness to do whatever it takes to serve. Let things play out and use every opportunity available to you. Again, do not feel you have to hide or keep quiet about your messages. They're real, you receive them. This has become a big part of your life. Certainly nothing to be ashamed of. Present them whenever you feel them to be useful. Do not brag—but humble in that respect. But be matter-of-fact. You were chosen for this—accept it and use it to further the cause of God and the Angels. Do not be overwhelmed by this. All in a day's work.

02/08/01

. . . You don't enjoy conflict. That is all right, speak when you wish, remain quiet when you choose to. You don't have to do anything. You know what you know. Others are frightened, you know that. Sharing your messages helps greatly in more ways than one. You do work with the Angels. We do give you guidance and words of great meaning—necessary teachings at this time. You are becoming more comfortable as time goes on. We see that. We knew you would. You have come far. Do not let skeptics about your words, your thoughts, disturb you, rattle you. Not everyone thinks

alike. Maintain your convictions, but be open to everyone. Listen to everyone. Then use the words you deem best—or no words at all. Sometimes it's better not to say anything.

01/30/01

. . . Your ways are not the norm, but they are becoming quite normal to you, are they not? You relate to God differently than most. You know that. The world needs you—needs more like you. Not afraid, or sometimes in spite of fear, to listen to the voice of God—and act upon it. You resonate with the word mystic. It suits you— you feel it—in your heart and soul. You recognize yourself. Yes, many can do this, but few are willing to take a chance to listen to their heart. What they miss! It's a shame. We have interrupted your lunch. Sorry, but you know when we have something to say—it needs to be received. Nourishment for the soul, so to speak . . . We will not steer you wrong—you know that. <u>TRUST</u>, <u>SERVE</u>, <u>LOVE</u>. You know that is your path.

These messages have been difficult for me to share. They are very personal, and I have always been a private person. I have been most comfortable being on the sidelines. So now, I have not only been asked to come out front, but to share much of my private self with others. The angels have spoken to me often of strength, courage, and bravery, and believe me, this takes a lot. But how could I refuse? For whatever reason, I have been chosen to receive these teachings and to reveal them. Their guidance in my life has been such an incredible gift, I could not deny this possibility to others. Hopefully, something in my story will resonate with you and cause you to turn to the wonderful guidance waiting in your own life. It is truly there for the asking. Trust me on this. But commit yourself to being open. That is imperative. And do not compare your experiences with anyone else's. We all have our own way—our own path to tread. There are many wonderful teachings out there, from many different sources. Don't limit yourself to what you have been told to believe. Listen to your heart. It gives you the truth. I sometimes joke that my way right now seems to be Taoist Christianity, and that's really not far from the truth. Taoism, especially the teachings of Lao-Tzu, so resonates with me. These teachings are so beautiful and take my thoughts far beyond anywhere I have ever gone before. My life has become so blessed with all of the wonderful teachings I have been exposed to in my reading. And my relationship with my angels and guides is beyond anything I can put into words. The connection to God that I feel, and my gratitude is so deep, that I will do my utmost to honor these gifts that I have been given and to fulfill the trust that has been placed upon me.

I would like to write briefly about the Goddess—the Divine Feminine. I will be brief because I suspect that I will cover this topic in-depth in a follow-up book. But I can not close this out without touching on it. Somewhere along the route, I became aware of the Goddess trying to get my attention. She is certainly nothing that I had ever considered before. I didn't truly think God was a man, but it was hard to get that childhood image out of my mind—the very old man with the long white hair and flowing beard who was looking down on us, and not very pleased. I had been told of all the things we did that displeased "Him." But I hadn't really considered God as a woman, either. However, I trust the messages, and messages about the Goddess were showing up everywhere.

I remembered that my friend Kevin had said I was like a goddess in his life. At the time, I thought that was an odd choice of words. Then I found out that I was born on the day considered to be sacred to the Goddess, Friday the 13th.

One day I was led to a sweatshirt in a department store. Trust me, I know when I'm being led. The sweatshirt had one word on it—GODDESS. Wow! Of course I had to buy it, but I certainly haven't had the courage to wear it. I asked the angels about it. Here is what they said:

10/17/00

> *It is our gift to you—to remind you of who you are—the She you are birthing—who will be used to help many others. Trust in what you are doing. Go with love. Us.*

I was reminded of two recent dreams. One was mine, the other was that of someone close to me. In them both, I was birthing a baby—in one, the baby was definitely a female. Okay.

Then on 10/28/00, I asked this question: "Can you tell me something about what I am to make of the "Goddess" in my life?"

> *You are to represent the Goddess on Earth. Do not be afraid of this. It is all perfectly natural. It fits in with all else that you are doing. You are a perfect choice—you who*

know how to love—in many forms—wife, mother, lover, friend, helper, server. This will apply. The Divine Feminine needs to be remembered. You are to help with that. There is so much beauty in the feminine— just look at you. You exemplify the Divine Feminine. She has been denigrated for so long. In that respect you are a Priestess— to serve Her—but not only that part—the feminine part—but all parts of the Divine Creator—masculine aspects too. A balance—that is what is needed. And things have been unbalanced for far, far too long. With your other duties (we hesitate to say duties, for this is your passion and your bliss), you will be expected to provide information (maybe a better word is knowledge) about the Divine Feminine. You have already begun. People will listen to you . . . So you can handle three aspects—Priestess for the Goddess, Disciple of Christ, and Healer with the Angels. Do not be daunted. This will come easily to you.

Oh, sure, this will be a piece of cake!

On 01/17/01, I received this:

God takes care of those who love Him/Her. We know, we can't talk to you like some in the past. You're very protective of your gender. As you should be. It's time someone showed the beauty and importance of the female spirit. We depend on your gifts and examples to always bring in the spiri-

tual aspect of things. After all, that's why we're here. To realize and understand our spiritual connection to God—to home. There are many from your past who love you and surround you with love. You are so blessed.

Maybe I wasn't as brief as I had intended, but there is so much about this that requires deep thought. I see God as being made up of both feminine and masculine aspects. We need to return the feminine aspects to their rightful place, alongside the masculine, making a whole. Then we will have reached a higher level of evolution. I will let the angels take you further with this in their teachings.

I would also like to leave you with one more perspective on my angels and guides. It is their humor. They have me laughing out loud at some of their messages. Two of my favorites, I would like to share with you. It is known in my family that my biggest food weakness is cake icing, straight out of the can. We do not keep it in the house. Recently, my youngest son, Alex, made a birthday cake for his brother, Mathew. The next morning I found a partial can of leftover icing in the refrigerator. The stuff is even better cold! I knew I shouldn't eat it, but I did. I ended up making it my breakfast. I knew I would pay the price. And I did, headache and all. Later on that morning, I was writing a message that ended with these words:

This will be the "icing on the cake." Sorry, play on words. A little problem with icing today? Learn from it.

On another occasion, they wrote:

We are truly a team, are we not—the "God Squad." Hope this offends no one—we thought it was "cute."

This had special meaning to me, as the Mod Squad was my favorite television show when I was in high school! I just wanted to share these with you to show that even though this is sacred and serious, it is also fun, at least my guides and angels are, and I enjoy spending time with them immensely.

On 01/27, they had told me that they would give me more information for a book—"stunning information" they had said. And on 02/05/01, I received this message:

Yes, we have much to do. Many teachings to impart. Thank you for accepting them. We are happy we have found such a worthy conduit for our teachings. So many will be helped and blessed by our words—by your words. Much is owed to you for your willingness and your abilities. So much to say, so many words to impart. You work hard. We are grateful. Keep up the good work—a book in no time. We will let you know when the time is right and help you to get it published. You are right to come forward at this time—teaching our words and ideas are important. You will do fine. Better than fine. Great. We have chosen well and love you so much. On with the work—so much to do.

True to their word, in early February, complete teachings began coming. I had gotten a few before, but now the push was on. A book was in the making. I would be given the topic and then the entire teaching at one sitting. I would be given them at various times, but one of their favorite times to impart this information seemed to be the middle of the night. I would wake up knowing the topic to be revealed. Sometimes I tried to negotiate—to get them to wait until the next morning. Usually they were insistent. Sometimes I would be too tired to even read over what they had given me until the next day. When I read it, I would be stunned. What I had been given was so incredible. These teachings are so beautiful, so honest, and so filled with love. I feel so privileged just to be able to read them. This past week they have awakened me numerous times. The other night I did request that they not wake me up, and they abided by my wishes. Usually, they give me the first sentence and I am hooked. One morning as I was waking up, I was given the title. This book was writing itself! I knew it needed to be made up of two parts—this part, explaining how all of this came to be—and the second part, containing nothing but their teachings. It was so important that I be a clear channel and I worried about it often.

On 02/13/01, I received this message:

> *Dear One,*
>
> *You assume too much responsibility for these messages. You do so well. You listen, you interpret, you convey our meanings. We rejoice in you. Give the responsibility over to us. You write what we tell you. Your ability to interpret our messages is phenomenal. Be assured. It is good to*

ask for clarification or corrections, but don't worry so much about the final outcome. These teachings are of major importance. We will make sure you stay on track. You are learning as we go along, aren't you? We relish your delight of our words and messages. It is good to have such a willing, passionate partner. God is truly pleased. Be assured. Go without worries and enjoy the day.

Before I finish up my part, I want to give you a bit of information about me—for you to connect with. I was born in 1951 in a small town in Southern Indiana. I am an only child. In May, I will have been married for twenty-eight years. My husband, John, is a physician, an anesthesiologist. We have made South Bend, Indiana our home for the past twenty years. I have a BA degree in Sociology. For the last twenty-five years, I have been a stay-at-home mom. I have always known that was a huge part of my path—the mom part. I never doubted it for a moment. However, traditional domestic skills do not seem to be a part of my path. I have two sons, Mathew, twenty-five, and Alex, soon to be fifteen. I also have a daughter-in-law, Colleen, who not only is like a daughter to me, but I consider her one of my closest friends, as I do my sons. I was certainly not expecting this in my life—who would? But the timing seems to be perfect, as God's timing always is.

I hope that my "confessions" and experiences will cause you to look at your own life differently—to be aware of the many signs around you—to experience your true connection to God. These teachings are filled with such love and hope and if we truly apply them, the world will become a much grander place, filled with the workings of the Spirit. We have that ability. All it takes is one person at a time, one moment at a time.

I wish to end with one more message. This will be the end of my part. The angels can speak for themselves and do in their part. Heed their words, please. You will all be the better for it.

02/20/01

You are doing really well. You so worry about misrepresenting us and also giving false information. You have such integrity—that's what makes you so trustworthy. You see each message as such a blessing. That makes our hearts joyful. It is natural for you to occasionally question our words or the way we choose to impart a teaching. We know what we are doing—but your credibility is on the line here. We understand that and value your concern. It is a valid one. We assure you that we always consider that in the giving. You are so precious to us—and valuable—that we consider this constantly. Do not fear. Again, no one will be harmed and many will be helped. You deserve much credit for your courage and willingness to present these to the public—people of all walks of life—of all faiths. You, we, will stir up controversy. More's the better. People need to be shaken out of their passivity, their narrow-mindedness. Even if they choose to disbelieve our words—at least they will have thought, have pondered another point of view. You are strong enough to handle the outcry. And you are so strong in your faith and knowing that you will stand firm. But be gentle and understanding of others. New ideas are hard to accept, especially when the old ones have been so entrenched for so long. Jesus the Christ is so pleased that you are presenting his teachings in this way—so full of love and encouragement. Be assured that he is working for your success in this mission. Much success is guaranteed. You also are a good and true servant and God is much pleased with you. More teachings are to come. Never fear. See if you can guess the next one. We'll give you a hint—it has to do with blessings. Wait for it and don't be surprised when it comes. You do so well, Linda. Be assured.

The
Teachings

THE TEACHINGS

BEAUTY
BITTERNESS
BLESSINGS
DEATH
DISSATISFACTION
THE DIVINE FEMININE
DIVINE GUIDANCE
EVIL
FAITH
FAITH-BASED ORGANIZATIONS
    and SOCIAL SERVICE
GOODNESS
GROWTH and LEARNING
HARM
HATRED
HEALTH CARE and ETHICS
HUMOR
LOVE
MAKING CHANGES
PAIN
PATIENCE
RAISING CHILDREN
SERVICE
SPIRITUALITY
TIME
TRUSTWORTHINESS
WORKING WITH THE ANGELS

BEAUTY

Look around you at all the Beauty. There is Beauty in everything. God is in everything. But Beauty truly is in the eye of the beholder. Make a commitment to see Beauty everywhere. This act will add additional blessings to your life. There will always be some things that appeal to you more than others. That is fine—it is a function of your humanness—your human personality—one of the things that makes you—you. But you can cultivate a stronger ability to see Beauty as it exists. Can Beauty only be recognized with the eyes? No, Beauty can be sensed—felt. It can be heard. Listen for Beautiful Sounds. They surround you. But often they are drowned out by the loud, chaotic sounds of everyday life on Earth.

Give yourself some time each day to focus on Beauty—of seeing it, hearing it, touching it, smelling it, and "feeling" it. Your life will be the richer for it.

Don't worry. Beauty won't go away. It can be found whenever sought. But too often, you turn a blind eye to Beauty. Don't you realize what that does to your Earthly experience?

Those who choose not to see Beauty are dour, sad, usually bitter people. But those who choose to see the Beauty that is there are joyous, and harmonious, and are a pleasure to be around.

Perhaps to be aware of Beauty, you need to allow yourself to be more childlike. Those are wonderful traits—to be open, excited, full of wonder. Most children are not yet surrounded by an awareness of the cares of the world. They need not be. But perhaps you need not be either. Perhaps you choose too many cares and burdens to surround yourself with. Some of these are your choice, you know.

So choose to see Beauty and surround yourselves with what appeals to you. Look to Nature—how much Beauty. In Nature, Beauty is rioting all over the place. Beauty in such abundance—and how harmonious—colors, textures, and smells all blending—a true feast for the senses. Take time to be aware of this. God's handiwork is everywhere, but no more apparent than in Nature. And you can learn much from Nature. Look there for important teachings. Resolve to learn the ways of Nature. You won't be bored.

And see the Beauty in every human being. There is no one correct way to look. Don't you see the constraints you put on yourselves by bowing to outside influence— usually those with their own agenda? You allow others to tell you who is beautiful or how to view the appearance of others. How is that possible? How can you give that over to anyone outside of yourself? Shame on you.

When will you learn to allow others to be themselves—not just allow—to encourage? To see the Beauty inherent in diversity—just like in Nature. You were not made to be so discriminating and so rigid—but humans have chosen that way. Now it is time to release those barriers. Barriers to acceptance—of others, of one's self. Acceptance creates harmony, balance, wholeness. Yes, it is wise to try to improve yourself—for yourself—for growth. But not at the expense of who you really are— and not when dictated by others. How can you possibly believe that one type, that one look, or one size fits all? That does a disservice to your Creator, does it not? Does it not imply that God was lacking in some way? How in the World can you imply that? But of course, you are of the World. Try to remember your connection to Spirit. Become more of the Spirit. You will then understand more—and see more of the Beauty in all.

And show others that you see their Beauty—you value them for who they are—you accept them—you embrace them. That will even bring out more Beauty—cause it to shine forth.

Make that your goal—to experience more of God's Beauty on Earth. Your life will be immeasurably richer for this decision. And if you so choose, you will not fail. Because Beauty truly is everywhere.

Walk forth today in Beauty and be made fuller. It is such a blessing. Cultivate it and encourage others in this quest. Shalom.

BITTERNESS

Bitterness is harmful to the soul. It fills the soul with darkness—crowding out the light—not the beneficial, creative darkness—the Void—the possibilities to come—but a soul destroying darkness—that takes much work to undo. Better to leave it alone in the first place.

Why choose bitterness—and you do choose it—you choose all of the experiences you manifest. Some things of life are so hard, so difficult to work through, to understand. You just shut down. Some go numb. Some choose bitterness. Either way, it's detrimental to your life experience. But bitterness is not contained within yourself. It seeps, spills out on others. Bitterness in someone is very noticeable—and drives away others at just the time you need them most.

There is no reason to choose bitterness at any time. Pain and hurt, yes—they come with some of your Earthly experience. But bitterness is a choice of darkness—and can destroy you and others around you. There is no longer any room for love, or hope, or trust, or courage, or strength. And you need all of those to get through the hard times.

Sinking into bitterness is the worst choice available. How can we explain the intense darkness of bitterness? The way it destroys your relationships. Earthly life is built on relationships—of your connection to others.

Again, we are not speaking about pain, or grief, or any natural response—that is temporary—not permanent. We are speaking of something that goes much deeper—a darkness that goes so very deep—that seems to take control—and does. Do not choose bitterness. Choose love and hope, whatever the circumstance. We are not saying this is easy—quite the contrary. But it can be done—and certainly is the preferred response.

Do not lose your life to something that is a destroyer. Take the hurts, the pain, the unbearable grief. Allow yourself to live with it—as long as it takes—learn from it—and choose to move on.

Many wonderful life changing experiences have come out of pain and grief, when the path of bitterness is not chosen—when the path of love and hope are chosen. Do not let any experience be in vain. Use it to grow—to connect—to feel love. And do not be afraid to seek help. Everyone needs help sometimes—we prefer you seek it often. Earthly life is made up of relationships of all kinds. Experience them. You will be the richer for it. Turn to God and the Angels in times of despair. We are here to love you and nurture you through the rough times as well as the joyful times. Share all with us, including your burdens. They will become lighter if you do. Trust us. And encourage those you love to release the bitterness. Do not give up without a fight. A fight that is filled with love and caring.

Love, caring, and hope can work miracles, you know. Nothing is ever lost. There is always a way to bring the light back. Seek it and you will find it. And don't give up—some results take time. Allow for it. We all experience situations differently—in our own way—our own time. Realize and don't expect too much—or use your timetable for others. Allow them their experiences. Their experiences need to be respected and allowed to run their course.

But surround them with love, encase them with love,

and the experience may be of less duration. And that is the desired way.

Life on Earth is hard, we know. You must experience it. That's why you're here. But you choose the way you experience it. Your responses are the deciding factor.

Choose love. Choose life. Make love your preferred way of living. You can never go wrong.

BLESSINGS

Blessings are gift from God. You don't have to do anything to earn them. They are just given to you. What is a blessing? Something that makes your life experience more beneficial. Something special along the way. That is what is usually thought of. But something can be a blessing without you realizing it. Something that at first glance seems to be negative—can turn out to be a great blessing. Again, judgement enters in. Some would say anything and everything is a blessing because it helps with your growth. Usually, though, we think of the special, the beautiful, the heart-lifting occurrence. Those we see as true blessings. Sometimes they are hoped for. Sometimes they are unexpected. They come in various guises. And very often they are recognized. People need to be aware of them—see them for what they are. So much is taken for granted in Earth life. But your life will be much richer, if you truly see the blessings in your life. And if you're one who thinks you have none or few, think again and look around. Blessings are everywhere—small to big. "See" them, if not with your eyes—with your heart. Learn to live your life in gratitude. A life blessed is truly one in which the person is constantly aware of his or her blessings.

Life on Earth itself is a blessing—a chance to be active, to create, to learn and grow from a variety of experiences.

It is said that because you are blessed—you are to be a blessing to others. Every one of you—can be a blessing to others. When you bless someone—they are brought face to face with the Divine in you.

Always strive to bring blessings into the lives of others. And ask for blessings upon others. That request is a beautiful gift—and one that can be bestowed for free—given by a longing of your heart. God listens, you know—and is delighted with the request. Make your request for others a daily occurrence. Just saying, "Bless you" or "Blessings" is a form of prayer. Those words, even if not spoken aloud, connect you to another and connect you with God. It shows your sense of the specialness, of the value of others. Because, remember, you are all connected, and when someone is blessed, it can be felt by all—it can have a domino effect—one blessing at a time.

And remember to be grateful for your blessings—for all that you receive—no matter which direction they come from. They are all gifts of the Divine, in whatever form they appear. Recognize them in your life, and you will not only be truly blessed but you will be able to bask in the warmth that comes with them.

So resolve to see them, and to provide them, and your life will be richer than you ever imagined. All for nothing—but yet, everything.

Bless you. You are so loved. Remember that, especially in your darkest hours. Go in PEACE.

DEATH

In reality, there is no death. You cannot kill a soul—a soul cannot die.

What we term death—is the soul leaving the Earthly human existence and returning to the spiritual realm from whence it came. The soul comes into a physical body to experience "life" on Earth. When that experience is deemed finished—the soul departs the body and the body "dies." Eventually, people will understand that there is no death. Jesus gave that example—that teaching—with his resurrection. People were to see—to understand, that life is everlasting—lasting beyond this physical realm.

It is very hard for loved ones when someone dies to the Earth plane. And it is an ending—in some respects—an ending to the previously known way of being. And lack of a physical presence is hard on those in the physical left behind. We grieve, we mourn, we learn to go on—but things are never the same. Change is a constant in physical life—ironic, isn't it? And we do create our own experiences—how we react to our life experiences. It is needed to be remembered that our loved ones have truly not died—that they are as alive as they ever were—more so—as they are experiencing a much fuller existence. They are the blessed ones. We need to rejoice for them. Their Earthly work is done. It is now time to rest up, then serve in another capacity. The learning and growing doesn't stop with the death of the body—just takes other forms.

And those left behind are bereft of love. The love continues, and those willing to be open, to take a chance, can still feel it on occasion.

Be happy for your loved ones who are experiencing the joy and peace of a job well-done and accomplished.

Know that they still love you dearly and have not truly left you. The love goes on and on. You <u>will</u> see them again when your Earthly work is finished. That is a promise if that is what you desire. Remember them in love and send prayers to light their way. You can participate more than you realize. Send love and prayers and gratitude that they blessed you with their presence on Earth. You are never alone. Love surrounds you in vast amounts. Feel it. Do not be afraid. "Death" is such a natural thing. It can not be avoided on the Earth plane but a person's life can be celebrated—should be celebrated. Continue to love. All will be well.

DISSATISFACTION

Dissatisfaction takes away from the peace of the moment—the inability to just enjoy what is. Envy enters in—envy of what others have. But not always—sometimes it's just really wanting something—thinking that will make you happy. Of course, happiness is found within. There are material things that pleasure you—that make you happy—more like provide enjoyment. Spiritually, they nourish you. Like, for instance, your lake house—it nourishes you spiritually—makes you feel good, peaceful, facilitates your work—relaxes you—enables you to think deeply, to connect with your inner spirit, and with nature. It makes you joyful. It is a beautiful thing to see. But you do not have to have it. Remembering your connection to Spirit is what's important—and your connection to others. What do you really long for? Your passion—if it is right and true—can indicate a part of your path, your mission for this life. Freeing yourself from the harshness of life can sometimes help with the work—if that is your chosen way. It depends on your goals for this lifetime. Sometimes you choose to learn through adversity. Sometimes growth comes from learning to be happy with what you have—other times there is something needed to propel you forward. The key is accepting—accept what you don't have—but also accept what is offered to you. Think deeply on this. You are able to feel what is right. Also, some things require sacrifices. What are you willing to forfeit or do without? But do not let lusting for things cause you to sacrifice your harmony—

your wholeness. Physical life on Earth is fraught with obstacles. Look inside for serenity. It can be found. Desire wholeness—your connection to God—above all and it will be obtained. Go in PEACE and SERENITY. We love you dearly. Meditate on our words and all will be well.

THE DIVINE FEMININE

The Divine Feminine is represented by the Goddess—but that is just another aspect of what people think of as God. Combining the two—God and Goddess, makes a whole—completeness—perfection.

People are again beginning to realize that God has two aspects or manifestations. Actually, people are beginning to understand this. That patriarchy and matriarchy were missing the other essential part. God is made up of both parts. It is necessary to blend the two to get a more complete sense of God. But even then—you can't imagine the wholeness, the Truth that is God. Humans do the best that they can at any given time. And that is alright. But now it is time to see both the feminine and masculine aspects of God/Goddess.

As we told you before, you are very protective of your gender—as well you should be. The Divine Feminine is so glorious. The world will function much better when those aspects are recognized. She has been missing for far too long. But She is being sensed, worshipped by many. One word of caution—you need the complete picture of God to find the completeness that will bring you peace. Honoring both the feminine and the masculine will bring a wholeness, a more accurate portrayal of God. What a glorious time awaits the human race when they recognize this and begin implementing the changes—the beautiful as well as the functional. Those who integrate both aspects will attain a much greater life than those who live by half. There is too much division in the human world. A blending—a bonding, is needed.

DIVINE GUIDANCE

Some call synchronicities the Voice of God. Coincidences with meaning are a form of Divine Guidance. There are no accidents, so one must tune in to what's going on. If you learn to tap into this guidance, to accept it, you will receive the Voice of God guiding you along your path.

As you know, the Angels are God's messengers on Earth. God is the source of the guidance—never fear. Angels can be the conduit between God and the Earthly realm. They work very hard to serve God in this way. Often they labor a long time with no results because the humans are not open—refuse to listen. But once an opening occurs, Divine Guidance begins to spill through. The more you trust, the more you are able to receive. And again, it is the messages, not the messengers that are ultimately most important.

Divine Guidance is trustworthy. True Divine Guidance will never steer you wrong, nor force you to do something. Divine Guidance gently propels you in the right direction. And sometimes guidance is given that we don't want to hear, but that we need to hear. And even that guidance is always given with love. No harm comes from Divine Guidance. The more you trust in it and implement it, the more you are able to receive.

Do not fear becoming too dependent on it—that won't happen. You will be told if that is a problem.

If you are honestly seeking guidance, and are open to it, you will receive it. Didn't Jesus say, "Seek and ye shall find"? God is always available and the true seeker will be rewarded with help undreamed of.

So, listen to everything, be aware of everything. You never know where your messages of guidance will come from. Again, the messages are freely given—the decision whether to follow the advice is up to you. And you will never be put in any position without support.

Your Angels and Guides love you very much. They are always with you—trying to help you, even when you are unaware. Honor and respect them, love them, and give them gratitude. They amply deserve it. God is well pleased with their work. Their service is truly esteemed. And you are well blessed to have them around.

Do not fear the guidance. It is for your benefit. Sometimes if you stray from your chosen path, they will remind you of why you are here.

Those who are aware of the guidance around them live better Earthly lives. Even the struggles are more bearable.

And remember, God loves you so much that you are given the beautiful, special beings as gifts of love.

Love them and listen to them. They are very wise and have your best interest at their heart.

You are so blessed. Amen.

EVIL

Evil does exist, you know, but not in the way you think. There is not a powerful being waiting, lurking, trying to draw you away from the good, from God.

There is no power that can compete with God. There is no way that the good of God can ultimately lose. But there are choices to be made. You live on a free will planet. In order to have free will, you must have choices. If you are only given one option, where's the choice?

In a situation of learning and growth, you must be presented with possibilities, different possible outcomes. You, alone, can choose your actions. But even if you choose what is considered to be the "wrong" possibility, you still learn from it, you still grow—eventually. It is desired that you grow immediately, or soon thereafter. But sometimes knowledge takes time to unfold.

But back to evil. There are bad choices, sometimes horrible, even seemingly unthinkable choices. These come by way of what we term negative energy. Remember there are 2 sides—the light side and the shadow side. Evil goes beyond what we usually term the shadow side. Evil causes harm—and harm is never to be desired.

Evil is an influx of massive negative energy. Evil takes advantage of others. It is an extremely selfish choice; one who is loving and kind never chooses an evil experience. But a choice, it is. And for it, consequences <u>must</u> be paid— and will be paid. Be assured of that. Justice must occur. Ultimately, that is left up to God—the workings of God. There is no way to truly punish evil adequately. Earthly justice can be administered—but be careful not to perpetrate your own form of evil against the evil-doer. And try to learn why—to understand why. And remember that the evil-doer is also a child of God, has a Divine Spark of God in him or her. Try to understand why that choice was made, so that such an evil choice can be averted in the future.

And try to maintain love in the face of evil. It can be done, but takes will-power, and not just self-will, but the will of God. Ask for help that you may radiate the love and light of God, in any circumstance.

And remain vigilant against evil—but not to the point of fear. Evil is not lurking around every corner, to tempt you away from God, just waiting for one tiny slip.

And be careful in your judgements as to what constitutes evil. Just because you have a problem with someone's choice, does not make it evil—do not label it so.

Do not get hung up on where this comes from. There is no mystery. The choice is made—for whatever reason.

The choice of evil means that someone is so very separated from the light—is living in such darkness. All beings need light shone upon them. That is your protection, to vow to live in the light—and shine that light on others.

Again, evil is the extreme. Negative energy is around in varying degrees. Most fairly benign—or seemingly so. But evil can be perpetrated by those believing they are doing good. Hatred and fear can produce evil choices. Stay away from those feelings. They can fester and eat up the good within. Do not use these as excuses for applying evil effects on others—even in the name of God. It has been done, you know.

And instead of worrying so much about what someone is doing, especially in the light of a choice that can be a poor choice, but not an evil one, look to yourself. Work on yourself, try to make of yourself an example of good—of making the choice of a loving God, of living the way of the Angels.

One of the most evil choices is violence—against oneself or another. Violence is not to be tolerated. Remember that in your dealings. And also remember that two wrongs don't make a right.

We hope we have made ourselves clear. This is another difficult teaching to impart and understand. We reiterate—stay away from violence—both mental and physical. Seek to always build someone up, not tear down. And always make sure that justice is meted out with love, not vengeance or in revenge. Vengeance always hurts the spirit of the one who chooses it. It is harmful. Try to learn true understanding and apply compassion within bounds. But also realize that "no one" made anyone choose an evil doing—it stems from the darkness inside.

Try to make the world a better place by resolving to always shine light and love. Can you imagine the positive energy around if many made that decision? It would be glorious. When there is light—there is no room for darkness. Look to yourself to provide it. It is your duty, is it not? Go in PEACE, and LOVE, and LIGHT.

FAITH

What is faith? Faith is when something can't be proven, but you believe in it—you know it to be true.

Faith is a state of the mind. You don't need proof—you just believe. Although, beliefs are something you choose to accept. Faith goes beyond that. Faith is a knowing—that something is—or that something will occur. Sometimes in spite of seeming indications to the contrary. The faithful are very important to God. They can be used to do good work—to bring God's love to others.

You can't see God—in the usual terms, but you can "feel" God and God's love.

Faith can move mountains. Harder still, faith can move men's minds—cause unbelievable changes. Faith replaces fear. With faith, there is no need to fear. Faith can be strengthened. Even a small amount of faith can accomplish great things. Faith works miracles. Ask Jesus. Miracles do happen. But you have to believe them when you see them. Don't discount them—or search for rational explanations. They aren't always to be found. Believe and then know. As Wayne Dyer has said—"You'll see it when you believe it." No truer advice given.

Keeping the faith can be difficult. Much on Earth tempts you to look away from faith. But never fear—faith can accomplish great things.

Faith is one of those gifts given by God to make life on Earth easier. Do not be dissuaded from your faith. Be Strong. Be Courageous. Be Sure. KEEP THE FAITH. AMEN.

FAITH-BASED ORGANIZATIONS
And
SOCIAL SERVICES

Question: "Do you have something to say about faith-based organizations helping with social services?"

Who better to dispense love? Because of their connection to God and their belief in the equality of human beings, and their knowledge of God's love for all, faith-based organizations give a special brand of helping. True healing is dependent on the spirit—wholeness. Government agencies can't necessarily provide that. Love can only be given when felt. You can't learn that, or pay for that. True love comes from the heart. Many groups are already dispensing love of a Godly kind. They deserve help. They are taking care of their fellow men and women. That also does not facilitate dependence on the state. It brings value and hope to many. They appreciate it. They feel cared for and loved—if even for a little while. George Bush knows the importance of this work. He understands love and compassion. He is such a moral man with great character. Be proud of him. He will do wonders.

No, it is not right to force religion on anyone, but to share God's love is necessary. God's love needn't be earned—it is there for everyone in abundance. Some religious leaders don't understand that. They have good hearts but are stuck in the fear-based teachings of the past. They truly believe they have to help others through fear. They are wrong.

Love, it's all about love. God uses others to shower people with Divine Love. Let it radiate through you. You have been chosen for this task. Remember—true love can be felt, recognized. It washes over others as a gentle rain—nurturing flowers and helping them bloom. Be afraid of imposed dogma——but not God-inspired love. There will be a new spirit of love in this country. Be assured. Good times are ahead—in spite of the bad times that are also ahead. Maintain your connection with President Bush. He needs people like you supporting him. People who love—for a living—or at least—for living. God's love can be counted on. People are wise who recognize it and accept it. Those who don't, truly miss out on something spectacular. But all will learn in time. You can count on that.

Question: "Do you wish to say more about the equality of human beings?"

Yes. Many, many believe that everyone is equal. But others do not—they are judgemental—and you find that in some faith-based groups. Especially those stuck in dogma that has been presented with fear and arrogance. There is no one path—and everyone is equal in God's eyes and deserving of God's grace and unconditional love. Some are discriminatory based on race, gender, sexual preference, and beliefs. That is not equality. Showing God's love and healing does not come from rigid rules for being given help. God's love is given unconditionally—just because the love exists and everyone needs love and is deserving of love.

The truly honorable organizations will be found and helped, and used as examples. Much help is on the way. There are many people like you out there—truly loving and caring. They will be allowed and used to help those less fortunate. Not through punishment or force-ful efforts but through pure and simple love. And people feel it. They know when it's around. Keep the Faith. Healing will happen. Much good can come of this. Believe.

GOODNESS

What can we say about goodness? The very word brings pleasure and serenity, does it not? Who doesn't know a truly good person—someone we wish we could emulate, but consider it impossible? Goodness is not impossible. You all have goodness inside of you, just waiting to come out. Let it out more often—let other people see it. It is very apparent—like a light shining around you—reflecting your glow on others.

True goodness stems from God and eschews evil. You can't be doing true good works and evil things at the same time. It is just not possible. So, if you focus always on the good, how can you go wrong? You can't. It is just not possible. Now, we are not saying that sometimes you don't slip up, or make mistakes. Of course you do. Everyone does. And that is perfectly okay. The important thing is in the motivation. Seek to do good—and you will be successful. Seek to do harm—and you will be successful. Usually. See the importance of motivation? Be aware of your motivation in everything you do, even the good things you do. What do you hope to gain from it? Will your spirit profit? Will someone else's? Those are both reasons for doing good. Eventually, you won't have to try to see the motivation. Good doings will come so naturally to you, that to do otherwise will be very difficult. But being aware is a good beginning—a way to train yourself. There is nothing wrong with training yourself to do good. Not everything comes automatically. There is much work to be done on Earth—much to work on—

much to learn. That is perfectly acceptable. That is where some are wrong in their thinking—that if you are truly close to God—everything is so easy. Multitudes of situations on Earth are not easy. What would be the point? How do you learn and grow from easiness? Of course, this does not mean that every situation should be difficult either. Once you have worked through a situation, and learned the lesson well, it becomes easier to choose rightly the next time something similar appears. Not that there is a wrong choice—but if you want to grow, sooner or later you must make a better choice. People are faced with different difficulties. What is easy for one may be difficult for another. So don't judge another's difficulties. Do not become arrogant in the situations that are easy for you. Instead, work on those situations that are difficult for you. They are your life lessons. And help others with theirs. You might even learn something for your effort. Remember to always look for the good in others—you will find it—and do your best to help them bring that out. You are still looking for a definition of goodness, are you not? Look for the light, for the love, for the caring, the nurturing, for the loving, the kind, the compassionate, the serving. In most cases, there you will find goodness. Seek to be around it. It rubs off. Honestly. Try to emulate the good around you. You won't believe how good you feel. And that's what it's all about. Because if you feel it—you share it—without a doubt. We promise. Like seeks like.

GROWTH and LEARNING

You are learning much through your relationships. See them as learning tools. You don't like to think in terms of competition—superior, inferior. Good for you. It makes you uncomfortable. No one is to compare himself or herself with another. The goal is to do the best <u>you</u> can in any given moment. If you disappoint yourself, learn from it, move on, aspire to do better in the next moment. Also, always take responsibility for your actions. Own what you have done, resolve it, and then you are free to move on with a clear conscience. As we have told you many times before, guilt serves no purpose, except negative feelings for yourself—sometimes even misunderstood. Throw away the guilt, learn from the experience, resolve it, and vow to try harder, to do better the next time. And show love—in every situation. Then you can't go wrong. But remember everyone makes mistakes. No human being is perfect. Do not let mistakes stall you or even stop you in your tracks. That is one of the big temptations in Earthly life. When you are stopped or stalled, there is no growth. No, that's wrong—there are growth possibilities in any situation, but the growth is stagnant—not moving forward as quickly as desired. Remember the two L's in every situation—LOVE and LEARNING. Look for both—no matter how deep you have to dig—and embrace the process. It is for you—your growing closer to the Ideal—to your wholeness in God—growing and learning the lessons inherent in Earth life. There are possibilities every day. So vow to move, to change, to grow—to not become stagnant, however tempting. But if you do, see the lessons even in that and work very hard to get out of that trap.

And ask God for help. God and the Angels are always here to guide you and support you. Learn to trust your instincts. The answers are given to you. Work to learn to "see" them, accept them, and be grateful—show gratitude for the help you have received. A loving, grateful heart will take you far.

HARM

About harm. Harm is not the same as hurt. Everyone hurts occasionally—physically or emotionally. Some we bring on ourselves—some we allow to happen. We must protect ourselves from hurt—to look at it, and move on. We are the ones that allow the hurt. We choose to have that experience. Hurts are temporary. Harm is much more serious—deeper. Harm can cause serious problems to the body, emotions, mind, and soul. Harm is never to be chosen. Harm is a deep wound—that requires much work to resolve, to overcome. Make it your policy to never harm anyone. Hurts happen—sometimes we can't control that. But to harm someone is an evil choice. Remember that. Be very careful on all accounts. Realize the sacredness of all human beings. The human body houses a sacred soul— one that is connected to God Almighty. Do not take that for granted or trivialize it. So, do your best to help those who are hurting—and try never to harm. Learn to discern the difference. Always practice love and righteousness. That is the way of God and the Angels. Always look for the goodness in others. It's there. And uplift those parts. Try not to be so judgemental. Learn to deal with your own faults and continue to love everyone. Remember, see both sides and you will do well. Also, remember to protect yourself from hurts. Only you can allow hurts to get through. Learn to shield yourself by the force-field of love around you and in you. Be assured of yourself and your path and mission. Persevere and deflect the barbs that come your way. You can do this. You are much stronger than you think. Remember the love of God for you and remember God loves everyone the same. Unconditional love. Never fear. We, on the other hand, hold a special love for you. We are here to personalize God's love—to work with you directly. We relish our task—not a task really, a pleasure. Have a good day. Walk in Peace and Serenity. All will be well.

HATRED

Hate is a by-product of fear. When fear is gone, there's room for love. The same is true of hatred. In a loving heart, there is no room for hatred. God does not promote hatred, neither did Jesus the Christ. Love—it's all about love. The main teachings were about love—loving God, loving each other as self, and loving your self. If you can do all of those—you have accomplished much. But temptations are all around—Earthly temptations that foster fear and result in hatred—especially possessiveness. Don't people understand—everything comes from God—is God? You can't possess God, but you can realize your connection to God—that is what makes you whole. So many fear losing something—losing things. "Things" can be beneficial—but owning them is not what it's about. You must learn it's all about love. And sometimes love means letting go of someone or something. That doesn't mean the love ends.

Ideologies and dogmas foster hatred—if you let them. It's all right to have beliefs. We encourage that. But you should be open to challenges. That makes you stronger. You are free to share your beliefs. But you should never try to impose your beliefs on anyone else. Force does not accomplish a greater good. Defending is different than imposition. You must weigh the strength of your values. Decide how best to use them, if necessary.

So many "things" foster hatred. Differences or perceived differences promote hatred in many. Can't they see that all are alike in God's eyes? All valuable—all deserving of love and respect and honor. Can't they see that? No, because many years of fear have blinded them to the truth. The Truth. In God—we are All One. We are to show each other love—promote love—promote healing. Only love truly heals. You can use technologies for healing tangible ills—but love truly heals the spirit. So, whenever you feel fear—send out love. Do not let it fester into hatred. Hatred is hard to get rid of, once entrenched.

And do not spread these teachings of hatred to children—pure, innocent souls—harmed in this way. So sad. That way, hatred is perpetuated indefinitely. Your job should be to foster love—everywhere you can. Obviously, there are times when fear is needed to protect someone. Listen to your instincts. But that is not what we are speaking of. We are speaking of fear and hatred due to people's perceived differences or threatened ownership. Move beyond that. It is good for no one.

HEALTH CARE and ETHICS

Life on Earth has evolved with much great health care. You've also reached a point where ethics more and more comes into question. How far to go—where to draw the line? There will be experts "studying" this situation—not all reaching the same conclusion. Again, the goal is to show love—and do no harm. That must be measured, weighed in the decision making. Also, the individual versus the many. Always remember <u>love</u>. The answer is not always evident and many mistakes will be made. That is all right—learning situations all. Usually no <u>harm</u> done. More and more—people must learn to listen to their hearts—deep within—then apply reason for a balance. Both are needed to make good decisions. The answer that is right for one may not be right for another. No two situations are ever the same. Each is unique with its own particular way of learning. Remember—Always Show Love—don't get hung up on ego or conceit. How best to show love? Guidance is always available—when asked for, when listened to. God's laws are Universal and not the same as Earthly laws. Granted, that makes decision-making more difficult, but also more promising as learning experiences. Think of the evolution that can be attained. You are blessed to be on Earth at this time. Cherish it—all of it.

HUMOR

God has a sense of humor, you know. It is truly Divine. We are speaking of humor that lightens, that cheers and uplifts. Not humor that is disrespectful or hurtful. There is certainly a difference. And people can "feel" the difference.

A sense of humor also helps us put things into perspective—reminds us to not take some things too seriously. It provides us a fun experience—reminds us to play. Play is essential in Earth life. There is such healthy play. Play gives enjoyment but also provides learning experiences. Sometimes when you are too serious—you miss the underlying point. But play can help you have clarity.

Lighten up. Many experiences have a light side—not all of course. Some are so very serious and are meant to be taken so.

And you should never use humor to hurt someone—to wound. That is malicious and always unacceptable. And do not pretend humor after you have hurt someone in a thoughtless manner—worse yet in a thoughtful manner.

Play is harmless—it provokes joy and wonder. Laughter is good for the soul, but also for the body and mind.

See the humor inherent in circumstances. That shows you're open to the good—not always looking for trouble.

We Angels can be humorous in our dealings with you—but never ridiculing. We love you unconditionally and wish to sometimes bring a lightness aspect to our dealings. Too much heaviness brings you down.

Seeing someone with a smile—a twinkle in their eye, a cheerful countenance is such a lift for people. That is another way to serve. To bring cheer into someone's life.

Cultivate this meaningful trait. It will not only be good for you—but everyone you meet. That is another way of sharing the light—a lighter way. God smiles upon you, you know.

Remember that, when things seem bleak. Try to find a cheerful thought, something that fills your mind with delight.

And don't be suspect of good, clean, honoring humor. Learn to see it for what it is. A way to put some fun in life. Remember, fun is essential to a healthy life—a productive life. And fun is good for the soul. So, live with occasional fun and play and provide that for others. There are so many things to provoke it. Look at God's world closely and realize the benefits of humor. Have an enjoyable day!

LOVE

Today, we wish to speak of LOVE—especially with Valentine's Day looming. There are as many kinds of love as there are people—each one is unique—to the soul. People tend to think of "romantic love," but that is a misnomer. True love is soul deep—felt at such a deep level.

There is the love of the Divine—the Ultimate Love— our true connection. Then, there is the love of our true soul-mate—the true mate of our soul—some refer to as twin soul, polar being, twin flame. This is the other half of your soul—the one you grow with, and come together with—when you evolve that far—when the soul evolves that far. This is felt on such a deep level—when you are ready, there is no mistaking it. Your whole being responds. There is the love you feel for souls you are to work with for good in this lifetime. Many you have known well before.

These are some of the very special loves on Earth. But the goal is to love all—unconditionally. That is God's promise—to love unconditionally. As above, so below. We must try to bring Divine Love to Earthly love. We are to share Divine Love with others—tangible evidences of God's love poured through other humans. Sharing God's love and light is such a worthy goal. We should all aspire to it. But to share love, you must feel love. God gives us love in many forms. Learn to recognize it and absorb it wherever it comes from—whenever it comes. Don't just rely on one person—one form of love. Love is in abundance all around. And remember to feel deserving of it. That is God's promise. You will be loved—no matter what, no matter who you are, or what you have done. The Divine Spark of God lives in <u>everyone</u>. Learn to recognize it and honor it.

There's room for romantic love—humans are to experience love in its many forms—but know that real love, true love is the ultimate. Find a way to love everyone—irregardless of Earthly laws or dogmas. Love can be found in every situation. Listen to your heart. Learn to suspend judgements and see God in every being.

Live your life the way that works best for you, not the way others tell you. You know inside what feels right. No one can force you to love or not love someone. You know what you feel. Honor that. Honor your journey—that takes you closer to God. Be yourself. You are worthy of love. Put yourself where you feel the love most.

Honor all of the relationships in your life. They are there for a purpose. So, even show love to those that confound you, or hurt you. See what they are teaching you—and send them love. Again, love the way <u>you</u> feel, not the way someone tells you you <u>should</u> feel. Each lifetime is a short journey—with much to learn. There are many loved ones with you. And remember, love never ends—just takes different forms.

Cherish all in your life and find the right place for them to fit. They will. Go in LOVE. Feel the LOVE. It is all around. Bless you.

MAKING CHANGES

Changes happen one movement at a time—not movement as in a group—but the movement by each individual moment by moment. Changes need to start small to be truly effective. That way they become ingrained and last. And most changes need to be wanted—sought—to last— to become a part of one's being. They should not be forced or brought about by ridicule. Respect everyone's process. Change by force is sometimes necessary, although rare, and only then to protect someone from harm. Show respect and realize that they have a right to be who they are, whether you like it or not. Realize, too, that you are all connected and that the movement of one affects the whole. Remember that as you go about your day—trying always to do good and show love. It truly can change the world. Remember—big steps in small increments. It is fine to put the wisdom out there—the impetus for change. Try to present it in a loving way, not a hateful way. And before you do, think about whether it is your place to do so. Making judgements is difficult to rationalize, sometimes. These ideals are not absolutes. There are extenuating circumstances. But usually this is not the case. It is usually one person or group trying to force their ideas on others. When that happens, where is the growth or learning? Or maybe something else was learned—not intended, and not as beneficial.

It is good to try to change the world for the better, but slowly, lovingly, one movement at a time. Go in LOVE. Think about what we have said. It is good advice. Know it.

PAIN

Unfortunately, you think—pain is a way in which you grow. You think it is undesirable—but it isn't. Pain is the way chosen to learn certain experiences—experiences that you must have in order to balance your training. It has been said before, how can you know joy, if you've never experienced pain? Pain though hurtful—does not harm. It is all part of the Earth experience. You should remember this.

And just because the human personality does not desire pain, the soul may very well choose that form by which to learn. Learn from these experiences. Then they will not need to be repeated. Do not go out of your way to cause pain for others—but know that occasionally you will. When people are working together—as you do on Earth—pain sometimes is a part of the process. It can not be helped.

Now for the flip side—joy—recognize it and embrace it when it comes. Embrace all experiences—however—and know that every aspect has a shadow side. True learning entails experiencing them all.

Provide love for those in pain, be empathetic, but know that you can't experience these aspects for them—you have your own agenda, as do they. Be supportive and loving and encourage them to work through it quickly—but thoroughly. When pain happens—know that there will be a new day to come which will contain brighter experiences.

Do not get stalled in the painful place. And as hard as

it will be, bless the paingiver—knowing that they have given you an opportunity for great growth.

Do not choose to stay in the pain experience. In order to move through it more quickly—recognize it, accept it, go into it, learn from it, and release it. The worst thing you can do is ignore it, push it aside. It will remain much longer and cause you repeated hurts. Do not be one who enjoys pain—who creates it continually. Pain is not an adventure—it is a lesson to be learned. Learn it with a joyful heart and move on.

We know this is a difficult teaching, but we have given you good and true advice. Also know that you are never alone. Do not suffer in silence. Surround yourself with help—from Earth and above—to help you navigate the road. You need never be alone—you are never alone.

In human terms, sharing these experiences brings you closer—fosters more connection among you. In heavenly terms—love, support, and guidance are there for you always. Do not reject the help, but ask for it, and accept it. It will lessen your pain. Experiences can be lessened through support and love. Always give it—but also receive—for that is the way—giving and receiving—another form of balance. Remember this teaching when the pain comes—as it inevitably will.

Do not fear it or await it, but go about your life joyously. There is plenty of time to deal with it, when it comes along. But a person who has cultivated the art of living joyously, will already have lessened the painful experience's power to hurt before it even appears. Good preventative medicine, we say.

Accept PAIN, but choose JOY. The way will be cleared—and the next experience will come. You choose.

PATIENCE

Patience. What is patience? The ability to wait—wait for the desired outcome. To go slowly—to let things unfold in their own time—their destined time. Know that if something is to be, it will be, and no amount of hurrying or worrying can cause it to happen. Earthly time means nothing in the higher realms. Those who reside there see a much bigger picture than those on Earth who focus on increments of time.

You've heard the phrase—"The watched pot never boils." Not quite true, but the principle is the same. You can't force something to happen before its time. To do so interferes with the scheme of things, throws difficulties in the way, and may actually hold up the outcome.

So, cultivate patience, knowing that it's out of your hands. Trying to direct it does not make it happen.

Now, that doesn't mean you are not to participate in the outcome. Quite the contrary. Do what you must do to set things in motion. This signifies your intent—then sit back and wait. Try not to worry. Worry is not beneficial, does much more harm than good.

Feel safe, knowing that you are protected, supported, and loved from above. It truly is in God's hands. Learn to relinquish control. You will feel better. Be aware of your connection with the Divine. Together—great things are created. Nothing is created alone, there is much help and support around you. Feel it. Understand it. Bask in it. You are truly blessed. Be patient.

RAISING CHILDREN

The most important thing you can do for your children—is shower them with love. Surround them with love—make them realize how special and important they are. Teach them of God's love for them. So they grow up never doubting how lovable they are—how loved they are.

Cherish them and be grateful for their place in your life. But never forget that each is an individual soul—bent on having their own learning experiences. They are here for a reason, as you are. Teach them and guide them and show them love—and never forget—you do not possess or own them. You can not own another soul. Only share their love space.

Be blessed by their appearance in your life. They truly are gifts from God. What an unimaginable honor—the opportunity to love and guide a soul at the beginning of his or her Earth experience.

If you truly show your children how blessed you are by them—they will in turn bless you. But you must also give them space—to grow on their own—in their way. Nurture them, but give them space to grow. You will be amazed by their full-blown beauty.

Accept them even when they make mistakes—as they will—one of the most effective ways of learning and growing. Mistakes are all part of the process—of life on Earth.

Do not confuse them with yourselves. They have their own agenda. You are only a part of it. There are many connections in their lives—many different types of relationships. Honor their journey, their growth, their experiences. Children are not just to honor their parents—and parents should strive to be deserving of that honor—but parents are to honor their children—as children of God—brothers and sisters in Christ.

Call it what you will, the relationship between parent and child in the Earthly journey is one of great commitment and great possibilities. Try to fill the role of parent in God's example—unconditional love, nurturance, guidance, and freedom—the freedom to Be. Honor that and you will be well blessed. Go in LOVE.

SERVICE

Your duty is to serve God. How best to serve God? To help one another. Service to your fellow man and woman is essential. Do not forget this. How can one hope to attain unity with God, without attaining unity with others? And how best to do that? With service. Realize your connection to others. When you realize that connection, you will see the beauty of others. When you see the beauty of others, you will see their value and know that you can do no less than to help them and serve them. By serving others, in whatever means, you are serving God. And God is well-pleased.

God feels unconditional love for all—even those considered to be the least. Remember the saying—"To whom much is given—from whom much is expected." Always remember that you are so blessed, you must be a blessing to others. This is not a chore to you, this is something you desire above all. You are not expected to do everything. You know your assets, how you can best serve God. That is what is expected, desired of you. You do make the decision, however. Try to use your abilities to make the lives of others a little better—giving them a feeling of value, of hope. Show them love.

Service is a beautiful vocation—much desired. Those with a strong connection to God know this. But again, people serve in different ways—their paths are different. Do not look in judgement on any soul. Their way of service may be to provide you with someone to serve. You can never judge another's path. That is why it is essential to serve others with a loving heart. God is so pleased with this. Remind people of their connection to God, in a loving way, not a forceful way.

There are so many ways of serving, expressions of service. They are all valid. Each one should choose the ones that are right for him or her. Try to serve someone each day. You'll be the better for it. Sometimes a smile is all that is needed, or a kind word. Not everything has to be grandiose. Simple gestures mean so much—especially when unexpected. God shows you the way. It is your choice to follow. Please do so. Many will benefit, including yourself.

SPIRITUALITY

Spirituality is about your connection to God. Based on the feelings and knowings of your spirit—internal—not on religious dogmas or restraints put on you by others—the external.

Spirituality encompasses many religions—but religious does not necessarily connote spirituality. You must learn to cultivate the stirrings of your spirit. Learn to listen and feel—for yourself. For that is how God speaks to you—in the quiet—within. Go within to listen and talk to God. All of the great religions teach this. Listen to your heart—and use your mind to balance—not the other way around. Learn to suspend judgement—be willing to follow the guidance and wisdom of your heart space. There are many great teachings in religions—and some not so great. Learn to discern the difference. They are apparent to the true seeker. Trust yourself. Trust God.

You do not need any external rules or restrictions telling you how to think—commanding you. You came here knowing it all—commit yourself to remembering. Everyone is on their own path to God. Encourage them with love and support knowing that no harm will befall them by their seeking. God loves the seeker—the seeker is open and that leaves an opening for God's wisdom and love to enter.

Always seek with love—not fear—and do not attempt to force your beliefs on anyone—and certainly not with the threat of eternal punishment. It does not exist. Fear-based teachings must stop. It is time to usher in an age of love.

God loves you—everyone. Know that. Be secure in that. And then you are free to seek—to fly—to soar. As Jesus said, "Seek and ye shall find"—not be told what to do. Honor the seeker—because at one time or another—you will be the seeker. Provide nourishment for his or her journey—support and love—sustenance—and refreshment for the weary. Much will be accomplished for both of you in that arrangement. And listen to others' tales of their journey. There may be a guidepost contained therein for your journey. Seek to find—but remember you already do know.

Go in peace and love, secure in the knowledge that God and the Angels are traveling right along-side of you. Do not be weary, but adventurous and practice acceptance along the way.

TIME

Time—it's very meaningless. But then again, it can be very meaningful. What do we mean? What goes on—what occurs in any given moment has great meaning. But the measurement of time it occurs in is very meaningless. It's the action itself—not the increment of time—the measurement of time—that holds the significance.

Time means little in the Spiritual Realm where "life" is lived in the "Now." Everything occurs in the moment. In the present moment you are not living in the past or the future. But yet they are occurring—are impacted.

What you choose to do in any given moment is extremely important. It will affect the future and can affect the past—the outcome. You impact the past by the meaning you attach to it in the Now—and that in turn affects the future. So, you are constantly creating in that respect. In different times—you might attach different meanings to what has already occurred—and that impacts the present. Therefore, the present moment is all you really have in which to create.

This is a very difficult teaching to understand. It's the action that's important—not the space of time in which it occurs. Time is a way to measure on Earth. But in reality, all is eternal. Every thought, every action exists. On Earth, it is helpful to see things in their measure of time—their space. For example, it is good to mark important events such as birthdays and important anniversaries with time, to facilitate our remembering and celebrating them. But it is the meaning of the event that is really important.

Meaning is more important than time. Time is just used as a marker.

Using time is helpful to make arrangements, to connect with one another, but it is the connection that is important. Remember that—it is the meaning that is attached to any given moment in time—that is worth remembering. Time is just an Earth tool. But since Time is used on Earth, try to be prompt. Your time is not any more important than anyone else's. Being "on time" facilitates the experience's success.

No amount of time is truly wasted. There is always learning and growth occurring. Decide how successful you want each moment to be. Be always aware. Live in the Now. You choose the meaning for the Now. Be discriminating in your choosing. Once gone, the possibilities for the moment are gone. Again, choose wisely. Act in a "timely" manner.

It's about the action, remember that. And if it seems there is no action—you are choosing that—and that in itself is an action. You have a choice in every Earth moment. Use it wisely in betterment of yourself or someone else. But if you don't, don't bemoan the loss of time. It's your decision. Do with it what you will. Time is pregnant with possibilities. You choose how you wish to use it. You have more freedom in this respect than you realize.

TRUSTWORTHINESS

Being trustworthy is the way of the Angels. Do everything in your power to keep your word. Live a life of value and honor and set a fine example for others. That is expected of you.

At this time on Earth, there is a dearth of trustworthiness. Too many people just think of themselves or those close to them and forget about others. The Truth is you are sharing the planet with many just like yourselves. America is a great country—founded on the ideals of God. It is time to look at those ideals again—to refresh your memories. The Founders knew what they were doing—they had a mission—to have a country based on freedom—what a novel idea! They put their heart and soul into this "great experiment." But you have wandered far from the ideal. Look around—where is the hope and love and look of fulfillment in the eyes of many that you meet? Too often, those looks are missing. Remember, all are valuable.

It is time to bring back trustworthiness. Keep your word. Honor your commitments. Allow others to turn to you in time of need. Honor yourselves. See the worth in everyone. Show the example of honor and integrity.

It is a new day in America, with a leader who can provide wonderful examples for its people. Watch him for guidance.

These things take time to change. Put away selfishness and think of others. Be firm in your resolves. Do your best in any given moment. That's all we ask of you—

all God asks of you.

WORKING WITH THE ANGELS

On working with the Angels. That is actually a misnomer—working. What we do is not always work—sometimes it's play—in good fun, of course. A sense of humor is Divine. Remember that.

You all have Angels around you, you know. We love you, support you, and care for you. We try to make things happen, sometimes, for we know the best workings to get things done. But we never interfere with your free will. Ultimately, what you do—your choice—is up to you.

We surround you at all times—for protection, for whatever is needed. God never sends anyone to Earth alone. That is a promise. More and more people are becoming aware of our presence. It is time. Much good can be accomplished when Angels are worked with directly—in full knowledge.

Who, or what are Angels? We are many types. There are the traditional ones people always think of. Those are beings who have never been on Earth, but remain in their own realm—the Angelic Realm. They have a particular point of view.

There are the Guides—those of varying abilities who are in between Earth visits—or who have moved beyond Earth life.

Advanced teachers are Masters—they have truly mastered the Earth lessons and have chosen to teach their Earth wisdom as a form of service. They have so much wisdom and knowledge and do delight in their work—as do all of us, actually.

Then there are departed loved ones. There are always some around to provide a different sort of support. They love you in a very personal way. All of the Angels love you—but these have been with you recently and know the ways of your current Earth personality. They also have feelings for you based on their experiences. If you could just feel their love for you—it radiates based on the wonderful Earth experiences you have recently shared.

So, we are made of many types, but we all work together to provide you with the best experience available. We call in whatever expert is needed at the time—whatever the problem or the need may be. We are always at your service.

Obviously, your loved ones mostly provide love, encouragement, and support. They rarely have the expertise needed for specific technical actions. That is left to the experts. You can count on that. But expert help would be sorely lacking without the love and encouragement you receive from those close to you on a personal level. All forms of support are needed and provided to truly help you with your Earth life experiences.

All we ask is that you let us help you. Stop trying to do everything on your own. If we allowed ourselves, we could get so frustrated at your stubbornness in refusing help, in trying to control and do everything yourself. But we also know that that is a very big part of the learning process of Earth. Save yourself some trouble. Turn to us in times of need—no matter how big or how small. We are here just for that purpose. God loves you that much. No one comes to Earth alone. Feel secure in that fact. And also feel secure that you can never do anything to cause God or us to stop loving you. We may get disappointed sometimes, but that does not affect our love for you. We will try to direct you to a better choice next time. Listen to us, please. Usually we are very quiet, but we are always there. Sometimes, we have to shout in an attempt to get your attention. The signs are everywhere. You still ignore us. But you have no more excuses. After reading this book, you know about us. You have been told—big time. Please listen to reason and let us help. You will certainly be the better for it—and you will make us very happy. And happiness is such a blessed feeling! Cultivate it—and it can be yours.

The author would love to hear from you. If you have comments you'd like to make or experiences you'd like to share, you may reach her at:

Linda Porter
Ascential Publishing Inc.
P.O. Box 4132
South Bend, IN 46634
E-mail: ascentialbooks@aol.com
Web: www.ascentialpublishing.com

Visit our website for ordering information. Personalized, autographed copies are also available.

Many blessings on you.